plain vanilla wrapper

gary skinner

vanilla publishing company

g skinner enterprises inc.

colorado springs, co

Published by
vanilla publishing company
g skinner enterprises inc.
3472 Research Parkway Suite 104
Colorado Springs, Colorado 80920
garyskinner.com

Edited by
Sharon Hancock

Designed by
Cathy Couchman

Layout by
Jonathan Gullery

Printed by
Books Just Books

Library of Congress Catalog Number: 2005925436

ISBN: 0-9767347-0-2

This book is dedicated to
My parents, Clarence and Lois Skinner,
Who, never gave up on me, or God.

In humor is sorrow
In sorrow is wit
In shallowness, profundity
In heaviness, delight
In pointlessness is pertinence
In weakness is potency
In dimness, hope
In honesty, liberty

Contents

Acknowledgments

You know who you are.
You know what you did.

Thanks.

Introduction

It was the spring of 2002, the last weekend of April to be exact, and I was scheduled to tell my story at a men's retreat. Nothing within me looked forward to it. You see, I don't like my story. In fact, I hate it. Yet over and over again in my quiet moments with God, He has impressed upon me that my story belongs to Him, and I need to be available to tell it when the opportunities arise.

At times I wonder if I am truly experiencing the heart of God on a matter or if I am conjuring up some hyper-spiritual feeling within me. In light of the fact that the things God showed me came to pass, I have more confidence in sharing what took place.

About a week before the retreat, I was out jogging on a favorite path. After twenty minutes, I got a picture in my mind of some men standing before me with tears streaming down their faces and terror in their eyes. It lasted for only a few seconds and then everything went back to normal. I found myself reacting out loud, "What in the world was that?"

Immediately, I sensed the Lord speak to my heart, **"Gary, that is what it is going to look like when you share your story next week.**

Let this be an encouragement not to back down when the time arrives."

There was a time in my life when I would not have put much stock in such a moment, but I have learned through similar circumstances over the past few years that this was God communicating with me. No, I did not hear an audible voice, but rather I had a clear impression beyond something I would normally think of on my own.

At the retreat, two strong thoughts came to mind:

"Gary, I want you to tell your story as if this is the last time you'll ever tell it. Hold nothing back."

And

"Gary, there is one man in the audience whose last chance is tonight. I've been trying to get his attention for a long time, and if he does not respond tonight it will be too late. He has hardened his heart over and over again to the point that he is losing his ability to be sensitive to my voice. Tonight is his last chance."

To say the least, this caught my attention.

I walked out on stage and literally poured out everything within me into those next two and a half hours. It was a holy moment. The presence of God filled the room. When I finished, I turned the meeting over to one of my associates and stepped out to get a breath of fresh air. While outside I noticed a man standing nearby, shaking and crying. He told me he knew he was the man with the last chance.

After a few minutes I returned. As I walked back into the auditorium I could not believe my eyes. There were bodies everywhere: on the floor, hanging over seats; men on their knees and on their faces. And I heard agonizing wailing, the kind that comes from the gut. I had never in my life heard men wail. I didn't know what to think.

As soon as the crowd saw me, a line began to form of men wanting to talk with me. To this day I do not remember what any of them said specifically, but I do remember that each one had tears streaming down his face and a look of terror in his eyes, as if it were Judgment Day. They began confessing their sins to me. Some had been carrying guilt and shame for several years.

The next day there were reports of all manner of healing. Father and son relationships were restored, broken friendships were mended, many made recommitments to Christ, and some even experienced physical healing in their bodies. What excited me most was that the "talk" of the day was not about me. They weren't discussing what a great story I'd told or what a great job I had done. Their conversation was about how the Holy Spirit had moved among us the night before.

In many respects, that evening has become the inspiration I've needed to follow through with putting my story in written form. To tell you the truth, I'm not all that excited about writing this down. Yet I feel compelled to do so because I've been told it will make a difference. Unfortunately,

I've lived most of my life thinking about myself and what I want and very little about what might be good for others. So, in reality, I am writing this out of a desire to help others...and in particular, to help you. I realize that last statement is more than a little presumptuous in that I probably don't know you...so why would I think I could help you? Let me say this: Somehow, some way, this story is going to impact you. It is about you, even though it's my story. Somewhere in here, something is going to grab your attention, and all of a sudden you are going to find yourself thinking in ways you hadn't thought before. Your heart is going to be stirred about some of your most inner, private, and sacred thoughts. In fact, there will be times when it will seem like my story is more about you than it is about me.

This is a about a journey...a journey with God. You may or may not even believe in God. What you believe does not affect the story. My role is not to convince you of anything. My role is to write down what happened and let you figure out whatever you need, for yourself.

I will say this: God is pursuing you.

Regardless of how old you are, what you've done in the past, or even what you think about God, it does not change the reality of this truth.

This story seems to have the flexibility to touch people in a variety of ways. For some it will be an encouragement to stay steady on the course they've been living. For others it will be a wake-up call announcing that He is still very interested in accomplishing things through them that they may have forgotten or given up on. For still others, this may be their last chance. He has been trying to get their attention for a long time and for whatever reason, they have allowed their hearts to become hardened toward Him. There is such a thing as our hearts becoming so hardened that we can't hear, see, or comprehend God's pursuit of us. This story could be a final effort to reach beyond that hardness so they might know Him in a real and personal way. I believe if they are still breathing, it is not too late.

Ultimately, this is a matter between you and God, so I'll do my best to tell the story, and leave the details between the two of you.

Chapter 1
Called of God

It was about 10:30 at night. My wife Susan and I were driving through Kansas on our way through the Midwest. As Susan slept, I was struggling to keep my mind on the task at hand.

How had things come to this? How had it gotten this far? How had I gotten in this deep?

We'd only been married a little over four years and I had managed to completely wreck our lives. I glanced over to my right to take as many quick looks at her as I could and still drive safely. She seemed so peaceful for the moment. Susan had believed in me, and in the midst of our dilemma, continued to act as if she still did. Only she and God knew the truth of her heart on this one, but every indication in her manner of speaking and actions communicated to me her undivided loyalty. A part of me wanted to pull over on the side of the road and watch her rest. I didn't want to talk anymore or explain anymore or process our circumstances anymore. I just wanted to be silent and soak in as much of her presence as I possibly could, because down deep I was fighting the fear that we were about to be ripped apart.

I'm sure everyone has at some point, said

some things they wish they could un-say, and done some things they wish they could undo. For me, it was too late for talking or fixing. Within the next forty-eight hours I would be standing in a courtroom, listening, as my fate would be stated, the consequence of some very foolish decisions.

In the stillness of night with only the sound of an occasional passing car or truck, my mind began to drift to those early years of my life. It was like a scene with Scrooge and the Ghost of Christmas Past.

At ten years old I was convinced God had put in me a desire, or a "calling," to serve in some form of full-time ministry like a missionary or a pastor.

Some boys want to be baseball players or policemen or the president of the United States when they grow up. It was not like that for me, because it wasn't about what I wanted, but about what God wanted. It was as if He had the rights to my life before I was given the opportunity to vote.

You see, for as long as I can remember, I've had tenderness in my heart toward God. In fact, I cannot remember a time in my life when I did not love Jesus. It was as if He was inside of me from the beginning. I must have spent half my childhood crying at an altar. I realize this sounds a little cheesy, but that's how it was.

Almost every Sunday the preacher would have an altar call at the end of his sermon. He would invite people to come forward for prayer for the purpose of committing their lives to Jesus or to receive forgiveness of some sin they may have committed. It was the Protestant version of "Confession."

I remember on one such occasion going up to the altar and being too embarrassed about my sin to say what it really was, so I lied. Well, I felt so guilty all afternoon that I could hardly wait for the evening service so I could go back up front again and ask forgiveness for lying that morning. I realize this sounds odd, but this is how a kid's mind works sometimes, which I think is fine because they should be allowed some freedom in such matters.

I also remember feeling sorry for the pastor at times because he would be preaching his heart out and some of the congregation would be falling asleep. Occasionally he looked a little discouraged, so at the altar call I'd go up front just to make him feel better. Of course he would ask me what I was there for and since I didn't want to tell him I felt sorry for him, I would make something up. Sometimes the cycle seemed endless.

The reason this is important is because I'm trying to give you a flavor of how things were for me in those days. I did a lot of silly things. Sometimes I would stand in my bedroom for hours on end singing hymns from one of the songbooks that Mom had around the house. I suppose part of the reason could be blamed on the way I was raised. Both of my parents were devoted to God and devoted to church. We had a rule in our house: "If the church doors are open, we are to be there." We went on Sunday morning, Sunday night, Wednesday night prayer meeting, every revival meeting, and seemingly, every special event. We were among the first to arrive and the last to leave. It was our life. To tell you the truth, I never resented it. I loved going to church. Even during my teen years I remained faithful. It was the place that I felt the closest to God, and I loved Him. That is probably why stories in the Bible about guys like Samuel who lived in the Temple sounded perfectly normal to me.

Some might think I was a sensitive kid. The truth is that I wasn't so much sensitive as I was hungry. I was hungry for God and the things that mattered to God. I'm not sure why some people have this hunger and others seem to be missing it. But I do recognize it's a gift, and if a person doesn't have it, I think they should ask for it. In fact, I think they should ask as often as it takes until they get it. God likes to answer such prayers.

Well, there I was in the very midst of one of my most hungry moments one Sunday when the preacher gave the invitation. "If there is anyone here tonight who feels they have been called to be a pastor or missionary, I would like you to come up to the front so I can pray for you."

Immediately I had a strong impression speak to my heart.

"Go."

It seemed like a lot of time had passed, but I finally got the nerve to take the first step. The next thing I knew I was all the way up front, almost as if I had been transported. I don't remember much else except that I stood there crying. (That's how I am when I feel close to God. I used to feel self-conscious about it, but since that seems to be my response to Him, I've decided to accept it.)

I knew God wasn't asking me to pray a little more or be on time for church or to drop a few extra nickels in the offering plate. He was calling me to come work for Him for the rest of my life, and in my mind that was the greatest honor there could ever be. I don't pretend to understand the ways of God and I definitely cannot explain why He would choose me. Yet, at that time, there was not even an inkling of doubt of the reality of the moment.

All seemed fine in the beginning. I was feeling pretty good about this new "call" on my life. It's kind of nice to know what you are supposed to do when you grow up. Most folks never know. They never figure out why they are here on this earth. They rarely end up doing anything but trying to make a decent living so they can have a few pleasures before they end up rotting in a grave somewhere. Most folks take the first thing that comes along that pays a decent wage.

There could be several reasons for this. Some people hate taking chances, so they grab on to something and don't let go until they get fired or laid off or decide to retire. Some just do what their dads have done for thirty years. Others do what their parents or friends tell them they should do.

Actually there is nothing wrong with any of these because all honest work is honorable. It is a shame in my mind, however, for someone to live in total discontent his entire life because of fear or confusion (which are probably two of the biggest reasons why people settle for less). Very few really have a clue as to what they should do, so for that I was fortunate. I did have a clue. I knew throughout my whole being. My problem was not in knowing, but in doing. I couldn't seem to follow through, even though I was so sure.

Where did those years of innocence go? How did I veer so far from that sureness, that "calling"?

My mind drifted back to the present. I was beginning to get tired of driving and knew this moment of serenity was about to end. Susan would awake soon. We would talk and process through possible outcomes of the next couple of days. I could hear Susan's questions in my mind before she ever asked them.

"Do you think you'll get probation?"

"Do you think you'll have to go to jail?"

"Do you think I'll have to drive all the way back home without you?"

"What will I do?"

"How will we get through this?"

Within every fiber of my being, I wished I could give her the answers that would bring her the peace and assurance she was seeking. But I didn't know what the outcome would be any more than she did. I had many of the same questions.

Chapter 2

Hints of Compromise

Rarely does a person's life flip from one direction to another overnight. Life is a series of opportunities, challenges, and decisions. This was definitely true of mine. I did not get myself in such a precarious position through one wrong turn. It was little by little, step by step. I do believe the better our heritage, the less likely we are to choose the wrong path. Yet, with all of my great influences, I was still able to defy the odds.

Although I spent a large portion of my time in those younger years involved in church activities, not all of life was about church. I did have other interests. One of those was work. I always enjoyed a good day's work, and still do. I would have to attribute that to my dad. Over the years he tried several occupations and owned some businesses. It never mattered to me what he did; rather his willingness to do what he needed to provide for us spoke volumes. In retrospect, he went through some pretty difficult times, but since our family was so great, life seemed wonderful from my perspective. Love in the home goes a long way. Oh, sure, I got my share of spankings and strong correction, but when I made a mistake, they encouraged me. Those are invaluable experiences for a kid.

Dad's work ethic rubbed off on me. I remember getting jobs mowing lawns, raking leaves, and delivering papers. I just assumed if I wanted spending money I needed to get a job and work for it. I did well for myself in those days too. Except for my first little venture.

I was six years old and decided to go into the sales business. I had just learned how to make a paper hat out of an old newspaper. I got pretty good at it right away, so I thought I could earn money selling them to neighbors. I gathered up all of our old newspapers and made about twenty-five or thirty hats. Even I thought they looked a little ridiculous when I put one on, but that wasn't about to stop my entrepreneurial spirit. So I tucked a few of them under my arm and started out door to door.

I felt good about my business during the planning stage. However, I wasn't prepared for how tough it was going to be out there in the real world.

I had picked a good day—Saturday—as everyone was home. All the elements were there: good profit, friendly prospects, and a wide open market. Hey, even the price was right, only one cent, and I had a good sales pitch.

"Hi, I'm Gary, I live a few houses down the street. Want to buy a paper hat for a penny?"

Yet I overlooked an important reality: my ability to fulfill need and want. So I went to fourteen doors and got fourteen rejections. Neighbors were nice about it, but no sales.

I started to get discouraged and my delivery began to lose its luster. Finally the big moment came. A tall, older man answered the door.

"What can I do for you son?"

"Hi, I'm Gary, I live a few houses down the street. Want to buy a paper hat for a penny?"

With great enthusiasm he smiled and said, "How about I give you a penny and you just keep your hat?" And he handed me a penny.

"Ok, sure...thanks," I said.

This should have felt like a great triumph, but even at the age of six, I knew I'd just received a handout. I ran home and threw my hat business in the trash.

As I grew older, I decided to take on jobs that were more physical. You know, the kind where you go to bed exhausted, but with the satisfaction of real accomplishment. That's what I experienced at the end of each summer day during my stays at Grandpa's. I loved those days. Of course, in my younger years I didn't do a lot of hard labor. It was just the event of getting up at dawn and staying in the fields till dark that gave me the feeling of fulfillment.

Grandpa was a great guy. He told some amazing stories, and I could sit and listen to them over and over again and never get bored. Rumor has it he stretched the tales at times, but to me that was part of the fun.

I loved tagging along with Grandpa, even if

we just drove his truck to town and back. Once in a while he let me drive the tractor, and that was about as grand as anything could be, since I was four years under the legal driving age. Most of the time he rode along with me, but now and then he let me do something, some small project, all by myself. Like drive out to a field and haul back a wagon, or drive up to the house for some water and bring it back to the field where he was mending fences. It seemed like there were always fences in need of mending.

I remember one time Grandpa told me to take the tractor and "go feed the cows."

It was a simple task. I was to drive the tractor to where he kept the hay. Load the hay onto the scoop on front of the tractor. Drive to a wooden bin and dump the hay in, repeating the process until two large bins were full. I had watched him do this dozens of times. It was no big deal. He had to run a quick errand in town, so this was my little project to keep me busy until he returned.

I felt grown-up to be trusted to do a job he usually did. Grandpa stood around for a couple of minutes to make sure I was okay. As soon as I completed the first load, he drove off.

The tractor was a John Deere. The steering wheel had a large knob bolted to it, so to turn, you could grab the knob and spin it around. It fascinated me to watch Grandpa do this, and I was eager to take full advantage of my opportunity.

The first few loads worked out fine. I did

everything just like he'd taught me. But somewhere around the fourth load I began to get sloppy. I decided to put the tractor in a higher gear and get aggressive with the steering wheel. In all my excitement I got carried away and whipped the tractor around too fast, only to find myself caught in a fence. The prongs on the front of the scoop got entangled in the mesh. A simple solution would have been to slowly ease the tractor backwards until the prongs were free. I didn't think of this until after I panicked.

In my state of alarm, I pulled back on the lever that controlled the scoop. Unfortunately, the lever caused the scoop to rise. The higher the scoop went, the higher the fence went. Before I knew it, about fifty feet of fence lifted right out of the ground, posts and all. I quickly jammed the lever forward. To my amazement, the fence dropped right back down in its original place. Relieved, I eased the tractor back out of the mesh. That could have been the end of my tractor driving days. The only problem was that fifty feet of fence now had a wobbly look to it. I decided to keep the tractor in a lower gear, take my time, and finish the job with a more humble attitude.

An hour or so later, Grandpa came home. I was sure he would figure out what I had done and put me on tractor-driving probation. But he never even noticed. Well, at least not at first. We were driving out to the field a couple of days later, which meant we had to drive past that fencerow. All of a sudden he stopped the tractor, stared at the fence, and said, "Now look at that fence, Gary. What in the world could have caused that?"

"Hmmmm," I answered.

I didn't look at him because I thought he would see right through me and somehow read my mind. I just kept staring at the fence like he did and said, "Hmmmm."

He didn't get off the tractor and inspect it any closer. He just started up again and said, "Well...I guess we're gonna have to get that thing tightened up."

I quietly sighed with relief and didn't say a word. Looking back, I should have just told Grandpa the truth. Sometimes, silence can be the biggest lie.

Chapter 3

A Change of Plans

As I moved into my teen years I was faced with some very important decisions. For example, should I be more involved in sports or music? These may not seem like critical choices, but if you look a little deeper, they can be determining factors of leadership and self-confidence. Pouring time and effort into a destiny of failure because of the lack of talent can be devastating to the future of any young person. Sure, there are those grand stories of the guy or gal who overcame incredible adversity, with little or no talent, to become a world champion. For most of us, however, those are nothing more than fairy tales. Fortunately in my case, it didn't take an overwhelming amount of disaster for me to catch on.

In my mind, these choices had nothing to do with ability. I had an idealistic outlook. I thought if I liked something, I should be able to do it. I was not a large kid in sixth grade; therefore, many sports didn't work out so well for me. I was too short to play basketball. I thought baseball was too slow unless you got to pitch, and I never got to pitch. All that was left was wrestling, track, and football. Soccer did not exist in our town. I kind of liked hockey, but it was too unpredictable because we depended upon a local pond for our rink.

So I made the logical choice.

After school one day I told my parents I could be in the band if I had an instrument to play. I didn't have a clue as to which one I should choose. My uncle offered me his old trombone for free, so I accepted. From that one snap decision, my future began to unfold.

I enjoyed playing the trombone in junior high and did fairly well at it. But when I entered high school, I decided to elevate my social status: I went out for football. At fourteen years old I stood 5'1" and weighed 115 lbs. I can't begin to tell you how great it felt to make the team, at least until I found out they didn't cut anyone. The school was small and they were just trying to fill the roster.

On the first day of practice the coach gave us some silly speech. Then his assistants passed out the practice gear. It consisted of a helmet, shoulder pads, a practice jersey, running shorts, and cleats. Since I was a freshman and one of the newest guys on the team, everybody else got their gear first. I got what was left over. The helmet was too big, the shoulder pads were too wide, and the practice jersey was pathetic. Most of the guys got jerseys according to their size. There were about six of us who got the "one size fits all." For the taller guys it was not a problem, but for me, that XXX jersey went all the way down to my ankles. As soon as I put it on, others began to laugh, "Hey Skinner, nice dress!"

I felt like an idiot. I thought to myself, *This doesn't make any sense at all. I'm going to trip over myself just jogging to the practice field.*

So, I walked into the coach's office and did a little complaining,

"Hey coach, this is not going to work. This jersey is way too big. Could you get one of the guys to switch with me?"

He looked down at me, paused for a moment, and said, "Nice dress, Skinner."

"Come on coach, I need a little break here."

"Quit your complaining, tuck that shirt in, and get on the field."

Well, I realized he wasn't going to give me any help, so I did what he said. The trouble is that tucked in, it looked even worse. It puffed out all the way around, giving the appearance of an inner tube in my pants.

As I ran onto the field, I looked down, only to notice my jersey had crept through the legs of my shorts and started hanging below my knees. It looked like I had tried to put shorts on over a dress. The toughest part came when I glanced to where my mom was watching the practice. She was almost in tears laughing so hard. You know if your mom is laughing at you, it's got to be bad. Lucky for me, she knew how to sew, and by the next practice I looked a lot less ridiculous.

It was a tough season and I only had one big moment. It took place during one of our practices. These practices could be rather difficult since the freshmen scrimmaged with the sophomores, juniors, and seniors. Some of those guys were huge. We would go through several drills on any given day, and on this particular day we were doing the "dummy drill."

Normally, I wasn't involved in this drill, but today was an exception. The coach called me over and showed me where I was supposed to stand. The stuffed bag was almost as tall as me and had a couple of handles on one side to hold it up. The guys on offense held the bags while the guys on defense "hit" the bags with their shoulders. Most of the offense lined up at the line of scrimmage. For some reason, they had me out in the middle of the field about ten yards behind everyone else. I began thinking to myself, *This is strange...why do they have me out here? There's not anyone across from me.*

About this time the coach blew his whistle and I watched the guys in front of me getting hit by the defense. About two seconds later, in my peripheral vision, I saw a guy running toward me at full speed. I thought, *No...that can't be my guy...he'll kill me!*

He had been placed about ten yards behind the line of scrimmage on his side, which meant that instead of hitting the bag from about a foot and a half away, he was getting a twenty-yard buildup. All I remember is closing my eyes and then gasping for air as I lay on the ground in agony.

I could hear everybody laughing, including the coach, who said, "Come on Skinner, get up, let's run that again."

I thought, *This can't be right. What is he thinking? Okay, it was funny once, but this is ridiculous.*

You see, the guy running me down was not only getting a good head start, but he was also the biggest, strongest, and most powerful player on the team. In fact, he was our only All-State candidate.

I caught my breath, got in position, and waited for the dreaded whistle. I knew now exactly what to do...close my eyes and pray.

Wham!

There I was on the ground again, gasping for air and writhing in pain.

I thought, *Okay, I made it. Everybody should be happy now.*

At least they sure sounded happy. I started to limp off the field, when I heard the coach say, "What do you think you're doing, Skinner? Pick that bag back up and get into position."

I began to get upset. I thought, *This stinks. This coach and this team are sick.*

But...I didn't want to be a quitter and I figured if I didn't stick this out, I'd never live it down. So I turned around, walked back across the field, picked up the bag, and prepared myself for the worst...again.

The coach blew the whistle and my opponent began running full speed, when all of a sudden, I got a brilliant idea. *I'm going to end this once and for all!*

Mr. All-State lunged forward with all he had.

His feet had left the ground when I stepped to the side and watched him hit the bag with no Skinner to support it.

He hit the ground so hard he knocked himself out. The coach came running onto the field screaming like a crazy person. "Skinner, what do you think you are doing? This is our best player. How could you do something like this? Get off the field!"

He and most of the team hovered over Mr. All-State. I stood on the sidelines next to the assistant coach. I felt bad for the guy, but I also felt relieved that I wasn't lying underneath the bag with his sweaty body crushing me.

Nobody laughed. In fact, everybody was mad at me for the moment. My only consolation was the assistant coach. He didn't look at me. He just stared straight ahead at the activity on the field. In a soft but firm voice he smiled and said, "Good job, Skinner...you did all right."

Though I survived football season, I realized I wasn't exactly cut out for the sport. Besides, I had a "call" on my life, which I kept on the forefront of my mind. Often I thought about that day in church when I sensed the voice of God speaking to my heart. But by the age of fifteen I got distracted. The culprit? Girls.

It's true that many teens succumb to drugs, drinking, and peer pressure. In my case, I obeyed my parents and never got in trouble with school or the law. Some would say I skipped the rebellious years. Instead my weakness was girls. I was a real sucker for some female attention.

Up until this time, I didn't mind telling everyone about my "calling." I was often asked, as all kids are, "Gary, what do you want to be when you grow up?"

"I'm going to be a pastor or a missionary."

Now things were changing. Now I was interested in girls and I wanted to impress them. I assumed the cute ones wouldn't think being a pastor or missionary was cool, so I stopped talking about it and stopped praying about it. As a result my enthusiasm waned. Then I started doubting "the call" and began thinking that being in ministry was a terrible idea. Eventually I concluded it was nothing more than a childish emotional response to a pastor's emotional invitation.

Somewhere between the ages of fifteen and eighteen I became extremely unsettled. God's calling on my life was still there, but my denial of it created an unconscious struggle within me. The only thing that kept me close to God was an incredible love for Jesus. I didn't once stop loving Him. No matter how lousy I messed things up, He never left me. Of course I didn't wanted Him to leave, I just wanted to lead my life, my way, and get His stamp of approval.

What I didn't understand is, why did Jesus stick around? If I were He, I would have left me a hundred times during the next several years. Yet He never did. That is why I believe if a person really gives his heart to Christ, no matter what, He's with the person for good. You might keep

Him pretty busy working you over until you learn a few lessons, but once He owns you, He'll go to almost any length to teach you those lessons. He's not concerned at all about time. He will use up your entire life to teach you one single thing if He has to. You might break His heart by your rebellion, but He won't give up on you. At least that's my theory because of how patient He was with me. Of course there's no guarantee you will last long enough to get turned around. There are a lot of people who die before they get it right.

People are dying every day and you or I might be next. Just pick up the newspaper. It is full of names of people who thought death was something far into the future, only to find themselves staring it in the face yesterday.

Aside from veering away from God's plan and going with my own, my life was okay. Not great, not horrible, but okay. You see, I wasn't an evil person and I didn't have evil plans. My heart was good, I loved God, and all in all, I was a decent guy. Yet, the longer I pursued my own plans, the more distant my relationship with God became. It was not anything sudden. It was kind of like having a best friend whom you talk to and spend time with daily, and then one day you begin drifting apart. There isn't a big argument. There isn't necessarily a particular event involved. You just develop different interests and priorities.

I still attended church, but I didn't "love" church like I used to. I still read the Bible, but it didn't have the life it used to have. I still hung out with other Christians, but we didn't talk about the things of God as much as we had previously. My relationship with God became more of a ritual of actions than an intimate friendship.

Being consumed with God is fine when you are young, I thought.

My senior year of high school became a pivotal point, as I decided to pursue music in a greater dimension. Probably the main reasons were that it was easy and it gave me a place of importance. As I mentioned earlier, I played the trombone. I was first chair from my sophomore year on, won several solo contests, and received a lot of recognition and "applause" for my efforts. In both my junior and senior years, I served as the band president. I felt important in my own circle of friends, a big fish in a little pond. I was president of my church's youth group, led worship for our church services, was the choir director, and often played solos. Yet, even then, I had one foot in and one foot out with regard to my commitment to God. Appearances are great with people, but you can't fool God. He knows what is really going on in our hearts.

Although I got off track from God's original plan, I still learned some valuable lessons about life. The issue was not really one of rebellion, but more of deception. I honestly thought I was on the right path. Of course, the problem with deception is deception. One cannot get out of deception when they are deceived because down deep they really do think they are right. Once again,

God knows our hearts, and in my case, He knew I was not plotting evil. I was just misdirected. He continued to be patient with me. I even found favor in most situations.

At the end of my senior year I was voted vice president of the honor society and won a partial scholarship in music to an Indiana state college. I graduated in 1973 with the respect of both teachers and students. The prospects for my future looked good and everyone, including myself, expected a fruitful, successful life for ol' Gary Skinner. Yet over the next three years I would become engaged in a downward spiral that would lead me on a path of destruction.

Chapter 4

The Future Looks Bright

We all want life to be tidy. We want to be able to reduce life's problems and issues into nice little packages. So when we try to explain "why" such and such has happened, we endeavor to come up with some practical, definitive answers. The truth is, life is not that simple. We seem to be consumed with seeking out "who" or "what" is to blame in matters that have turned our lives into less than what we wanted or expected. Yes, there are often times we can point to a particular instance or decision that is clearly a contributor to our dilemma, but more often a combination of decisions or actions are involved. This is exactly what happened in my case.

The fall of 1973 was the beginning of my freshman year at college. I was going to become a band teacher. Nothing glamorous, but I saw teaching as a great avenue to affect other kids' lives, as well as a way to be involved in music, something that was a growing passion with me. I hadn't been attending college very long, however, before I found I did not like it. I thought the reason was the fault of the school, the faculty, and the music program. In reality, the unsettledness was continuing to stir inside me. I chose to blame my circumstances rather than consider that I could be the problem.

My roommate that first year was a guy named Pete. He was great. He was intelligent, kind, disciplined, and a very talented classical guitarist. Being freshmen, we didn't get the best rooms available on campus. In fact, our room was in the basement right next to the laundry room. At first I thought this was a great convenience, but soon realized it was a curse. Whenever it was warm enough to have the window open, we would be engulfed with the pleasurable smell of dryer exhaust, which left me with a difficult decision. Did I want to experience a little cool air with the stuffy smell of drying clothes, or an uncomfortably hot room filled with the pungent odor of Pete's shoes? Most of the time I would opt for a compromise; keep the window shut, open our door to the hall, turn on a fan, and make Pete keep his shoes on.

Pete and I were complete opposites. You could count on him being at his desk studying diligently, writing letters home, reading a book; or being in a practice room somewhere perfecting his talents. I, on the other hand could be found watching television, playing pool or ping pong in the rec. room, or just hanging out with the guys at the music building who were supposed to be practicing. Pete carefully watched every penny he spent. I spent every penny I had on late night pizza cravings and jazz recordings. Pete often thought I was too carefree. I always thought he was too serious. I think we each had within us a secret commitment to change the other. He would nag me about my wasteful and bingeing habits. I would make sure he was exceptionally hungry and then order a pizza and eat the entire thing right in front of him. He would tell me I'd never amount to anything and I'd tell him that no matter what he accomplished he'd always be a bore. We became great friends.

By the time Christmas break rolled around, I started to put some serious time in the practice room, limiting my television viewing to the weekends, and actually preparing a couple of days in advance for some of my exams. Pete was going in half with me on the pizza and started showing up in the rec. room from time to time. Sometimes I'd get him laughing so hard he almost choked. Once in a while he'd get me thinking about purpose and commitment.

There were, however, some things Pete could not understand about me. One of those was my discontent with the college. By spring I was complaining more and more and found myself spending too much time with others who had the same views. Here's a good lesson: If you complain about something long enough and loud enough, pretty soon all those who think likewise will begin to gravitate toward you. Once you are surrounded by a couple of friends who think the same you will have unknowingly started your own club.

You'll talk about the school's weaknesses, the faculty, the food—anything and everything will be subject to criticism.

Next, fewer and fewer people want to be around you. But you probably won't notice, because as long as you have at least one other person who will join your club of "judgment," you will conclude you have an elitist understanding of things the other "robots" just don't have the insight to comprehend. You will begin to think you are more enlightened than the rest and therefore your criticisms are completely justified.

Now, I am among the first to say it is wrong to go along with the crowd just for the sake of doing what everyone else does. At the same time, I believe it is wrong to be "different" just for the sake of standing out. Both extremes have their pitfalls. I didn't interpret my situation as pertaining to either category. I actually thought I did have more understanding and it was my responsibility to change something. Either the university would have to change or I would. It was obvious which of the two it would be. I began to investigate the possibility of either quitting or switching schools.

As I reflect on that time in my life, I am startled by my immaturity. Yet, if I look a little deeper, I believe it ties into a lack of focus and direction, which was lost as soon as I sidestepped "the call." I've heard it said before that a missed bus could change the course of a person's life forever. I can't say much for busses, but my choices in those years impacted my future dramatically.

One day Pete said, "Gary, I have been thinking about going down to Bloomington to visit my girlfriend at Indiana University for a couple of days. Since you have a car, I was wondering if you would be willing to drive me down there. I'll pay for the gas and find us a place to stay."

"You mean a road trip?" I said.

"Yeah, sort of..."

"Why not? It would do me good to get out of here for a few days."

We made the arrangements, packed our bags, and headed off for the weekend. It was spring. All the trees were blooming and the grass was green. It was one of the most beautiful times of the year, so when we arrived at the campus, its majesty overwhelmed me.

While Pete was off talking to his girlfriend, I decided to take a stroll. After about an hour, I stumbled upon the School of Music. It was a natural place for me to land. By now the band teaching idea had lost its luster, and I had recently been considering a different major: "performance." I was thinking it would be a grand thing to play the trombone in an important orchestra somewhere in the world, or work in a recording studio, or maybe even travel with a jazz band like Stan Kenton or Woody Herman. Regardless, the reputation of Indiana University's School of Music was no secret. I had heard a lot about how great it was, but had not really considered it a possibility until that day.

I'm going to transfer, I thought to myself.

Several of my friends had talked about transferring, but they all said the same thing, "It's tough to get accepted down there."

"It's a whole different world."

"The competition is too stiff."

I didn't think much about it before. I just accepted their theories as fact. But now that I was visiting this campus and had seen the School of Music, there was no question in my mind about what to do. I needed to make my move and make it quick. I was sure there had to be some deadlines for transferring in time for the fall.

I decided to visit the admissions department. I walked in, explained to the secretary what I wanted to do, and she told me to have a seat and the admissions director would be happy to speak to me for a few minutes. I only had to wait perhaps ten minutes before Mr. "G" invited me into his office. I walked in, we greeted each other, and he said, "Well, Gary, how can I help you?"

"I am currently a music student and I would like to transfer to Indiana University. I really like it here and I think it would be better for my future if I could make the change."

"That would be great, except you'll have to wait another year."

"Another year? Why?"

"Well son, you missed the auditions by about two weeks. We've already processed those, so you'll have to wait until next year."

"Hmmmm."

Then I got a brilliant idea.

"What if I transfer without being in the School of Music and take my prerequisite courses, and then audition next spring? That way I'll already be here and it will just be the formality of me qualifying in the audition."

He didn't seem to be very pleased with this revelation.

"That's a terrible idea. What if you fail the audition?"

"I'm pretty sure I'll pass, and it's worth the risk to me."

He shook his head and sat back in his chair and stared at me for a couple of minutes.

"Gary, I don't want to discourage you, but I think you're being very foolish. This is not reasonable thinking."

"Well, it makes perfect sense to me, so I guess I'll see you next fall."

He stood up and said, "Gary, I think you are making a terrible mistake."

I took the hint and left, but not before I had the last word.

"Thank you for your time Mr. G. In most circumstances I'm sure your advice is correct, but I'm a little different than most."

He just shook his head and closed the door behind me.

Although I tried to leave the impression that all was well, down deep I felt rotten. I'd spent most of the day getting my hopes up and now they were dashed to pieces. I talked it over with

Pete on the way home. He thought Mr. G was making a lot of sense and transferring would be a poor decision. I talked it over with some friends when I got back to school and they all said the same thing. I talked it over with my parents and they too agreed.

So, after much thought and consideration, I decided to make the change anyway. Four months later, I arrived at my new residence, Indiana University.

About the second day there I was walking across the parking lot when I spotted Lewis Van Haney. Mr. Haney was the trombone professor that I was hoping to study under the following year after I passed the audition. I got his attention and asked if he had a couple of minutes. He said he was in a hurry, but could give me two minutes. I quickly told him the whole story, and then gave my best sales pitch about how much I wanted to learn from him and was there any way I could take lessons from him on the side?

"I'm sorry, Gary, if you are not in the School of Music, it's just not allowed."

"You mean you couldn't even let me pay you out of my own pocket for private lessons? We could do it off campus or something."

"Well, I suppose we could do that, but do you realize that it would cost you $35 for a half-hour lesson?"

"Oh."

That was way out of my budget. I realized the door was closing fast. He must have seen the disappointment on my face, so he said, "I'll tell you what. Come by my office on Monday at nine o'clock and let me hear you play. I've got a couple of grad students who could take you on, and one of them could get you up to speed for your audition in the spring."

I stood there staring into space, trying to process his idea.

"I'll listen to how well you play and that will help me determine which student to assign you to...okay?"

I was feeling less than at the top of my game for the moment, but I didn't want to let on that anything was wrong. Besides, he was being pretty helpful under the circumstances, and at least he wasn't' giving me the "you're an idiot" treatment that I had anticipated.

I practiced like a madman over the weekend, hoping for the best on Monday. I knew first impressions were often critical, so I wasn't going to take any chances by just going through the motions. Plus, I thought, *If he likes how I play now, he'll already be on my team somewhat by the time spring rolls around. I've got to do this well.*

I walked into his office on Monday and he asked me to play a few scales. Then he had me go through a piece I had prepared. It wasn't much of an audition. He kept cutting me off. I would start playing some scales and he'd say, "Hmmm. That's enough of that."

With my prepared piece, I was only able to get through twenty or thirty bars before he said,

"Hmmm," again and then gave me the ol' "That's enough."

At first I thought he was being rude. But then I reminded myself of how I had pushed myself on him and I should be thankful he was putting up with me. He finished by saying, "Gary, you can put your horn away, I've heard all I need to hear. Why don't you go over to my schedule board and sign up for a lesson time?"

"But sir, I can't. Remember? I'm not in the School of Music."

"You are now."

"I don't understand. I haven't had my audition yet."

"You just did. Don't worry. If I say you're in, you're in. That's all there is to it. Now go upstairs to the admissions office and ask for a Mr. G. Tell him you need the paperwork to make it official."

"I have a hunch he might not believe me."

"Gary, just do as I say...and if you run into any snags, have him call me. I'll be here all morning."

I thought, *You'd better stay close to your phone, because ol' Mr. G will want to talk.*

I immediately ran upstairs. I was so excited, partly because I could hardly wait to see the look on Mr. G's face. Well, I told him just like I was supposed to, but I made sure I did it with a tone of humility. I knew it was going to be rough enough on him to have to suck it up in front of some college punk, and there was a part of me that was still unsure if what had happened was really legitimate. He responded predictably, scolded me for not listening to him the previous spring, told me this was not how things were done around there, and proceeded to pick up his phone. I told him he should contact Mr. Haney.

"That's exactly what I'm going to do."

I stood there while he made the call. It was pretty pathetic. He started strong, but I could tell things were not going well for him as the conversation continued. I was beginning to feel a little sorry for him. I thought perhaps I should put my arm around his shoulder and reassure him that all would be fine. "No hard feelings, I'll put in a good word for you down at the office."

Of course, I didn't. That would have been arrogant to say the least, and since grace was flowing so plentifully in my direction, there was no reason to foul it up.

Chapter 5

Getting Distracted

The next few months were some of the best times in my life. Not that I had been living in some horrible oppressive environment, but there seemingly was a sense of joy and purpose awaiting me every day. Although I had moved away from "the call," my heart toward God was still very tender. In my mind I was not in a state of rebellion, but of doubt. I wasn't sure any longer that God had "called" me, but if He did, I saw my new career direction in music as a part of ministry. Music is often incorporated in a person's effectiveness in ministering to others. In a round about way, I convinced myself the path I was on was just another piece to the puzzle.

That first year at I.U. was going well, but by the end of the second semester, I became restless. I couldn't quite put my finger on it as to why, but I became bored with the whole college scene. I felt like a lot of the required classes were totally irrelevant. No matter whom I talked with, nobody was able to convince me that those courses were anything but "filler." It seemed to me the university system was set up to keep a lot of professors employed. Take that kind of thinking, mix in unsettledness and a dash of independence, and you've got a good recipe for change on the horizon.

I wish there was someone else to blame for my sporadic behavior, but there isn't anyone to accuse. There may have been a few who fueled the fire, but ultimately, all the decisions were mine. I did find a comrade in my friend Archie, another music major who was a decent saxophone player. Arch and I lived in the same dorm and we usually ate lunch and supper together. This was ample opportunity for us to complain and strategize a solution. Arch and I both had a fascination with California and the "Tonight Show Band." We both liked to watch Johnny Carson and Doc Severinsen as we were growing up, so when Arch posed the idea of getting off this university "merry-go-round" and trying our skills at playing our horns on the West Coast, I was excited.

The original plan was for each of us to work hard over the summer break, save our money, join up the following fall, and head out to Los Angeles. Once there we would each get a regular job, find an apartment to live in, get acquainted with some of the musicians in the area, try to establish ourselves, and hopefully get some playing gigs as we worked our way up. Although the idea may sound somewhat ridiculous on the surface, we did not have any grand illusions that any of this would happen quickly. We talked for hours about how it might take five to ten years to get ourselves known and established. Taking this into consideration, our plan really wasn't all that unreasonable. We were young, we had some talent, so with a little persistence, why not?

I worked pretty hard all summer and by the time it ended I had saved up $300 and enough for a bus ticket, one-way to L.A. I called Arch, who was living in Virginia, only to find out he had changed his mind. He said he didn't get much saved over the summer and he was going to return to I.U. This was a huge disappointment. I had thought about it, planned it, and had all of my hopes built over those three months to go west, so when he backed out, I didn't know how to react. My parents were not all that excited about my plans, so when they heard about Arch's decision, they thought they were off the hook.

They were wrong. I decided to go anyway. The adventure side of me just wouldn't give it up. I remember them sitting me down and trying a diplomatic approach to convince me this was a poor decision. Yet at the same time, they could see my determination, so I think they must have thought if they just let me go, I'd get this out of my system and be back soon. Besides, this kind of behavior was in my history. My grandfather had left home at age fourteen to join the circus, and my dad had joined the navy when he was young. My guess is that behind closed doors things were said like, "What do you expect, this restlessness is in the family."

I had never been a rebellious kid, so this new turn of events was more than a little startling to my parents. I wasn't mean about it, just determined. So, there I was, nineteen years old with $300 and a bus ticket heading off to a place I'd never been, without knowing anyone in the entire state of California. I got on the bus and road fifty-six hours to Glendale. That was one long trip. Believe it or not, I did have a plan. I was to arrive in the early morning so that I wouldn't be wandering around L.A. in the dark. I had also found out before I left that I could stay at the YMCA for about twenty bucks a week. The only glitch is that they didn't take reservations and there was a possibility that there wouldn't be a room available when I arrived. This, however, was not the case. All went well. I remember lying down on my bed that first afternoon after arriving, feeling rather proud of myself.

I didn't do much that first day except try and get caught up on some sleep. I got up the next day thinking I needed to get a job right away, so I picked up a newspaper and started looking. I circled quite a few options, but I didn't settle on anything. I wanted to get the lay of the land before I jumped right into the job-hunting fray. I went for a walk to check out the city and began to make some plans as to where I would like to find an apartment and what I might be able to afford. I also needed some planning to make sure I didn't run out of money, especially before I got a job.

As the evening approached I decided to find a decent place to have an inexpensive yet nice dinner as a reward to myself. I found a small place near the Y, ordered a steak, and relished the moment. Just as I was leaving the restaurant, an odd thing happened. A guy got out of his car, walked up to me, and said, "Hey, buddy, are you new in town?"

I thought to myself, *How in the world did he know that? I must look like I'm lost.*

"Yeah, I just got in yesterday."

"Let me buy you dinner then," he said.

"Thanks, but I just finished."

"Well, maybe some other time."

"Yeah, maybe some other time."

I started to walk away, thinking what a strange thing to have happen, when he called out to me again, "Hey, buddy, do you have a job yet?"

"No, I'm going to start looking tomorrow."

"Why don't you stop over at Barclay's department store? I think they are looking for a new clerk. They are one of my clients; so let me know if you're interested. I can put in a good word for you."

"Sure...I'll stop by tomorrow and check it out."

"Oh, by the way, my name is Raymond."

"I'm Gary."

"Great, maybe I'll see you tomorrow."

"Yeah, sure."

The whole incident seemed more than a little odd to me, but then again, I thought, *Maybe this is the way things are in Southern California.*

I went on my way and didn't really give our conversation much thought until the next day when I was sitting in Barclay's filling out an application. I was almost finished when Raymond walked in where several of us were waiting to be interviewed.

"Hi Gary."

"Hi Raymond."

"I've got an appointment with the boss right now so I'll put in a good word for you."

Then he winked at me and walked right in. About ten minutes passed, he walked out and winked again and said, "Don't worry, you've got the job."

Sure enough, when I went in the boss asked me a few simple questions and hired me on the spot. I didn't see Raymond again until a week later. I was walking in the store to go to work and there he was dressing some manikins.

"Hey Raymond, how are you doing?"

"Great, how about you?"

"Yes, everything is working out pretty well. By the way, thanks for helping me get this job."

"No problem."

Then he offered me his phone number and said, "Listen, if you ever need anything—a ride, some advice, anything—you can call me and I'll help you out."

Once again, I had an unsettling feeling come over me, but I just ignored it and thanked him for his offer. I didn't have anyone to talk to so in one sense this seemed like a great opportunity for me to make a friend. On the other hand, he might turn out to be a real bore, and then I'd have to start making up excuses for why I didn't want to hang out with him. It was better to just keep things the way they were.

In just a week I began to get low on finances. It was one of those situations where the company doesn't pay you for a couple of weeks. I had also been encouraged by the ol' YMCA director to find a more permanent residence. He said this was supposed to be a very temporary arrangement. So I set out to find a reasonable apartment. Glendale was not the best place in the world to find a deal, but after looking for most of the weekend, I finally found something suitable.

The apartment looked fine from the outside in that it was above a row of stores in a respectable area of town. The best part was it was only a couple of blocks from where I worked. The down side was the apartment itself. I had to walk up a steep, dingy stairway to the second floor. At the top of the stairs was the landlady. She was nice enough, but looked like she had lived a tough life. She wore an old flowered dress that looked like it might be one of only two or three options from her wardrobe, and this one was on its fourth or fifth day in a row. Her breath was disgusting because she was a chain smoker. She reminded me of one of those old pictures I'd seen before of a woman from Kentucky or Tennessee, leaning up against a wall, smoking a pipe. She walked with a cane and rarely smiled, but when she did, it was not much to look at since she only had about four teeth left, and they were brown.

I told her I didn't have enough for the full

month's rent since I had just arrived and wouldn't get paid for another week. She said I looked like a nice young man and though she rarely allowed such an arrangement, agreed to let me pay the rest of the rent with my next paycheck. It was only a two-room apartment. There was a living area with a tub in the corner and a very small kitchen. I didn't think much about it because all I needed was a place to lay my head at night and a stove and frig to manage my eating habits. There were no dishes or utensils, so I decided to go shopping.

I sat down and examined exactly how much money I had and how I was going to get by until my first check. I bought one knife, one spoon, one bowl, two loaves of bread, a gallon of milk, a box of pre-sweetened cereal, a jar of peanut butter, and a jar of strawberry jelly. I took the groceries home, sat down at the table, and created a schedule of exactly how many bowls of cereal and how many PB&Js I could have each day until my next check. If I were at home or in college, I would have been the biggest complainer you'd ever heard. But since it was my idea for this adventure, I actually felt gratified that everything was working out so well.

I suppose most folks would have been lonely, but for me this was about the best experience I had ever had. It felt good to know I'd survived with so little money and no one to help me. To pass the time I rode the bus over to Beverly Hills or Hollywood to investigate how the wealthy lived. I walked a lot and I prayed a lot. Not in desperation, but just hanging out, talking to God. I might add that I was not listening to Him too much, just talking.

This went on for about two months until one day I woke up and it was as if I had been hit in the head with a brick. I was bored. Some of you might think it was just the newness wearing off. I'll admit, that may have contributed to the situation some, but I think it was God answering my parents' prayers. I would call home once a week according to my pre-arranged agreement with them so they didn't worry too much. Dad was kind of funny. He'd always listen to my rambling on about how great it was in sunny California, but as soon as there was a lull in the conversation, he'd give me his sales pitch.

"Gary, why don't you come home? It has got to be difficult getting around out there without a car. Why don't you come back here, work for me, save some money, buy a car, and then go back when you are better off financially?"

I would always laugh to myself because I knew exactly what he was trying to do. When the boredom settled in, his ideas began to sound quite tempting. Sure, I had my own apartment, but it was kind of dumpy. I had a job, but it was meaningless. And his suggestion about the car was very appealing. Riding the bus was getting old. So finally, I took him up on his offer. I told him it would take me a few weeks to save up for a ticket, but he interrupted and said, "Your mom and I will send you a ticket. Just come on home."

As great as the adventure had been, it felt terrific to go home where I was loved and wanted. A few days later I received the plane ticket, one-way of course. I started making plans for my departure. It wasn't that easy to get to LAX from where I was living, so I thought this to be the perfect time to call on Raymond and bum a ride. However, when I dialed, it wasn't Raymond who answered. The guy on the other end said he'd heard of me and he would pass on the information to his roommate. About two hours later, I called again and Raymond answered. He said he'd be glad to help me out and give me a ride to the airport. The only catch was I had to agree to have dinner with him at his house. That seemed reasonable, so I agreed.

He picked me up the next day and we drove over to his apartment in North Hollywood. It wasn't a very large place, but was definitely much nicer than the slum I had been living in. As soon as we walked inside Raymond introduced me to his friend.

"Gary, this is Harold. He's my roommate and he's prepared a great dinner for us."

Harold was kind of spooky looking. Not like a vampire or anything, just a little strange. His hair was long, gray, and in a ponytail. He looked like a sixty-year-old hippie. Not that such a thing is necessarily good or bad, but in this case I just didn't feel comfortable around him. He was friendly, but there was something about him that made my skin crawl. We sat down for dinner and all I could think about was getting out of there and on the plane. I thought, *Just my luck to get myself cut up into a bunch of pieces by some nut the day I'm trying to get out of town.*

But that was it. Nothing happened. We made some small talk, ate our supper, said our good-byes, and headed off for the airport. Raymond insisted I look him up if I ever returned to L.A. I said, "Sure, why not?" Within a few hours I was home and the incident was all behind me.

The whole California excursion had been a good escapade, but it wasn't over in my mind. I vowed to return, more organized and better prepared financially.

Now there's a great little subject all its own, "vows." They are the strangest things. They seem to work against you on both sides. If you vow never to do something ever again, sure enough, you end up doing it. If you vow you will do something, "no matter what," for some odd reason it just doesn't seem to happen, unless, of course, it is a vow to do something that will make your life worse. Those almost always get carried out. At least that's what I've learned...the hard way.

Chapter 6

A Fork in the Road

Once I returned home I started working for my dad, bought a car, and tried saving some toward moving back out to L.A. Yet something still didn't seem quite right. One day, out of the blue, I got a revelation.

"This is no way to live my life. I need to get back to school and finish my education."

So I filled out the paperwork and re-entered Indiana University the following fall. It was great to be back at I.U. Mr. Haney was more than a little happy to see me, and everything seemed to be falling into place. It was as if I hadn't taken the previous year off. Just as before, favor was rampant.

This was wonderful and lasted about six weeks. All of a sudden I just couldn't stand being there anymore. I felt confused about what I wanted to do with my life. I once again became discontent with my classes and the direction of my future.

Archie and I found each other and the old talk about California resurfaced. In our private conversations we decided to quit school after Christmas break and fly to California together. He was resolute about going this time. And me? Well, I had done it once; I could do it again. I decided, however, to improve my trombone skills so I would have a better chance of "making it." To accomplish this, I committed to spend the remainder of the semester practicing like I never had before. Except for my music classes, I stopped attending everything.

I got up every morning at five o'clock, showered, ate breakfast, and arrived at the music building by six to begin my routine. I played the horn ten to twelve hours a day. I was told that playing a brass instrument more than six hours a day would turn a guy's chops into spaghetti, but that didn't deter me. Except for getting an occasional bloody lip, all went well—very well. I improved at an amazing pace. It was partly due to the time invested, but to a larger degree in *how* the time was invested.

I determined what everybody else hated to practice, and then rehearsed those things more than anyone else. For instance, I found that playing long tones, scales, and lip slurs were the disciplines musicians hated the most. So I began my day by playing these for an hour each. I used the rest of the time to practice assignments given by Mr. Haney. In doing so, I discovered a great principle that applies across the board: If you want to be successful at something, find out the most disliked aspect and become the best at it. It will move you ahead of the pack quite rapidly.

That is exactly what happened to me. Now

keep in mind, nobody knew what I was doing. I didn't tell my friends, Mr. Haney, or anyone else. This was my little secret and I thoroughly enjoyed the looks on everyone's faces when they heard me play. Mr. Haney was almost beside himself. You see, it was normal for a musical piece to be assigned at the beginning of the semester. The student would work on it over the next few months, and then, hopefully, have it in presentable form by the end of the semester. How well you did on your piece determined your grade.

In my case, Mr. Haney assigned me something one week and I performed it almost perfectly the following week. It blew his mind. I continued on my disciplined path of practicing long hours for three months and steadily improved. Then the big moment came for me to inform Mr. Haney about my plans for the future. I thought the best way to let him know would be to send him a letter from L.A. after I was out of town. It was the chicken way of handling it, but avoiding conflict was a strong character flaw of mine in those days. However, I decided to be more honorable and break the news face-to-face.

I'll never forget my final trombone lesson. When I walked in his office, he was sitting at his desk as usual. He smiled and said, "Gary, you don't need to get your horn out today. I have something I want to talk to you about."

I sat down and listened.

"Gary, I've been around this business for a lot of years, and I know you are aware that I played for the New York Philharmonic Orchestra for almost twenty years. I believe if you keep listening to me and improving like you have this year, you could make it into one of the big orchestras someday."

You can probably imagine how uncomfortable I was feeling. Nonetheless, I blurted it out. "Thanks for the encouragement, Mr. Haney. I really appreciate what you've said, but I'm not coming back next semester. I'm going to L.A."

He didn't say anything. He just slumped down in his chair and stared at me with a worried look. I felt uneasy with the silence, so I spoke up.

"Look sir, I have a confession to make. The only classes I've been attending this semester are ones related to music. I've been practicing my horn all day, every day. I'm going to flunk every class that's not a music class. The university is probably going to kick me out as soon as my grades are posted."

He sat up suddenly and said, "Gary, don't worry about your grades and the university, I can help you work through that. Just come back next semester. You are making a terrible mistake."

I just looked at him. Not in a mean way, but with a look of finality. He knew from that look I'd made up my mind. He'd seen it before. He remained calm, which was probably the best he could have offered at the time. When someone is convinced of an idea and a lack maturity is involved, nobody is likely to change the person's mind by telling him how stupid he is. It is very difficult for older adults to keep their mouths shut when younger adults are set on doing something foolish. Of course, when you are young and you are the one making the poor decision, you often think, *What's the big deal? It will all work out fine. Why don't the old folks mind their own business?*

I was talking to a gentlemen the other day who has been mentoring and teaching leaders for more than thirty years. He said, "There are three things I've never seen in youth—those under thirty. I've never seen patience, humility, or perspective. There may be glimpses at certain times, but they aren't present in a substantial way."

That was me: no patience, no humility, and definitely no perspective. I walked out of Mr. Haney's office that day feeling like I needed to take a shower. I didn't feel very clean about how things had ended.

Well, the semester wound down about two weeks later and Arch and I had our plans in place. We had made the arrangements for plane fare, what we were going to do when we arrived...all the significant details necessary to make this adventure as smooth as possible. Everything came together quite well, actually, and the excitement built in both of us. I had only one loose end to take care of and, in my mind, it wouldn't be much of a problem. At least that's what I thought.

Chapter 7

Losing Innocence

Arch and I were each going home for the holidays, which would give us plenty of time to convince our parents this was the right decision at the right time. Arch never said much to me about his parent's reaction other than, "Aw, they'll get over it."

Since I'd been through this once before, I didn't foresee any resistance other than a little chat about, "Are you sure this is the right thing to do?"

My assumption could not have been more wrong.

Instead of asking their opinion or permission, my plan was to state it in a matter of fact fashion. I didn't raise my voice, I just told them how it was going to be. "Mom and Dad, I'm not going back to school next semester. I'm going to L.A. instead."

As soon as I said the words "L.A. instead" a very sick feeling formed in the pit of my stomach. Probably not as sick as the pit in their stomachs, but nonetheless, confidence did not sweep over me. I don't remember what Mom said. She may not have said anything. What I do remember is the expression on my dad's face and the tone of his voice as he looked me in the eye and said, "Gary, you are not going. I will not let you. I am not going to let you throw your life away like this. You're going to put this craziness out of your mind and go back to college and finish your degree, and that's final!"

I had never seen him so animated and angry about anything as he was at that moment. Well, I had something brilliant to say to ol' Dad, "I'm twenty-one years old and you can't tell me what to do. I've made up my mind and I'm going, whether you like it or not!" It became very ugly after that. No, he didn't yell or hit me, he just turned and walked out of the room and never said another word. As odd as it may seem, that was the worst response I could have received. Down deep within me I knew I had terribly violated our relationship. And that is where I believe it all began. The curse was on. No, I don't believe he cursed me. In fact, he never said much about it again. He talked to me the next day as if nothing bad had happened between us. He never indicated any less love for me. Yet I believe I set some things in motion that I didn't realize until years later. I believe I cursed myself.

You see, there are a lot of great instructions in the Bible, all of them good. Then there are the Big Ten. You know, the tablets and Moses. I'm sure you've heard of them. I would never recommend anyone ignoring any of the commands in the Bible, but especially the Big Ten. These commands were put there to help protect us against ourselves. So when we break them certain dynamics take place. In my case, I had just broken number five, which says, "Honor your father and your mother."

It didn't matter that I was twenty-one. It would not have mattered if I were a hundred twenty-one. As long as my father and mother were alive, I needed to honor them. In fact, I believe I should continue to honor them whether they are around or not. This kind of logic may not set well with you. Maybe you believe like I did that once a person reaches a certain age, he has the right to do whatever he wants without the approval of his parents. Trust me, this is not the clearest of thinking.

Some of you have been wondering for years why your life seems to be such a mess, why you don't have any peace in your heart about who you are and what you are doing. You might even feel like you are under some kind of curse because no matter how hard you try, things don't work out well. I'm not saying this is the only possible reason, but it is worth considering.

You don't need to beat yourself up if you have dishonored your parents. It is actually easy to fix. All you need to do is ask God to forgive you, then go and ask your parents to forgive you. This will take care of both sins: the sin against God, who set up the rules in the first place, and the sin against your parents. Just get honest in your heart about the matter, and tell God you are sorry for breaking number five and how rotten you feel about the whole mess. He has a way of making everything we foul up turn around for good.

Perhaps your parents have already died so you can't apologize to them. Do whatever it takes to get your heart clean. You might have to visit their grave; not so that you can have a conversation with them, but it might make you feel better. Some theologians would say that I'm crazy on this one, but I say, "Do whatever you need to do to get free."

God will not judge you for being honest in your effort to righting your wrongs. Actually, just the opposite is true. I am convinced He is eager to forgive. God is not only able, but is very much in favor of helping you get back on the right track. Honest repentance pleases Him greatly. You will be amazed at how quickly the curse will fall right off of you.

As for me, well, it took over twenty years to figure that out. One of the most amazing features of my story is how I could live under a curse for so long and not get myself killed. I'm not sure why, except perhaps God honored the prayers of my parents, who still loved me and prayed for me. What I don't want to do at this point is give you some sense of false security. Over the years, I have seen several people get bumped off early in life. I'm not saying dishonoring your parents is the only reason, but He did promise long life if we obey number five. It is definitely something to think about. Why risk it any longer? Why not just deal with it before God and move on? At the very least, you will experience the benefit of a cleaner heart.

So there we were, Arch and I, on a plane to Los Angeles: our heads full of big ideas and our hearts full of hope. We had left behind our youth and were now about to lose some of the innocence that goes along with being young. We were about to be forced to grow up, fast. This new life in L.A. was not going to give us preferential treatment based on our age.

We arrived at LAX with $600 each and no real clue as to where we would stay first. I had told Arch about my old friend Raymond and so the consensus was for me to give him a call and have him pick us up at the airport. Raymond suggested that we take a shuttle bus from the airport to the Holiday Inn in Hollywood and he could pick us up there. That seemed reasonable, so we hopped on the shuttle and arrived about an hour later. Raymond picked us up and drove us a few blocks away to a cheap motel. He said he knew the manager and helped us get a discounted rate for a week's stay. That would give us enough time to scout out the area and find an apartment.

I felt pretty important in front of Arch since I was the one with a local connection. I had taken care of things quite well and Arch was very appreciative, at least until he met Raymond. The entire time I was thinking to myself, *This guy sure is nice. We're very lucky to have a friend like this to help us get a few things figured out.*

Arch saw things in a different light. In fact, as soon as Raymond got out of the car to talk to the motel owner, Arch pulled me aside and said, "Get rid of your buddy, Gary...now."

"What's the problem? He's just trying to help us."

Arch moved close to my face and said, "Get rid of him. He's got other plans."

"What do you mean?"

"Gary, he's a homosexual and he's got more on his mind than being your local registered best friend."

"No...you're kidding, right?"

"No, Gary, I'm not kidding. Actually, I can't believe you didn't pick up on that before."

"But Arch, he's such a nice guy. Are you sure?"

Arch said, "Think about it for a minute. Remember when you first met him, how he was so eager to get to know you and help you out? Do you think he just picked you out of a crowd because he wanted you to feel welcome in sunny California? Trust me, Gary, this guy has plans for you. I suggest you get rid of him in your good ol' boy nice manner before I get rid of him in mine."

I thought about it for a second or two and decided it would be best if I did the talking. So I politely told Raymond we were very tired from the trip and hoped he didn't mind calling it a night. After Arch's comments, I have to admit the picture became clearer. This new revelation explained several of Raymond's past remarks. All of a sudden I shuddered. I had never before seen myself as someone to be taken advantage of. The pieces began to come together. Thinking about Raymond making advances toward me and setting me up made me feel more than just a little uncomfortable. I thought, *Why would someone do that? Aren't all people basically good?*

I was thankful to have Arch and some of his "street smarts" with me on this trip. Arch had been raised on the East Coast and had faced racial discrimination in his own life, so he wasn't prejudiced about Raymond, he just felt it his duty to watch out for me. In fact he even said more than once, "If Raymond wants to live like that, I suppose it's his business, but he better not try and make his business my business."

I was awfully naive in those days. As I recall, Raymond didn't come around much after that.

Our next two biggest challenges were to find a place to live and to find jobs. We looked around for a couple of days at different apartments and finally settled on a studio apartment on Franklin Ave. It had two couches that each unfolded into separate beds, a very small kitchen, and a bathroom. The carpet was long orange shag. The place didn't look like much, but at least it had air-conditioning and the price was right, $165 per month. The truth is, it was more than a little dumpy, but when you're young like we were, it becomes a part of the adventure.

As far as employment, Arch wanted to find something where he could wear his three-piece suit every day. He had this thing about wearing a suit. Sure enough, he was able to land work as a teller in a local bank. I had other plans. I wanted to have a car, so I started looking around for jobs that might provide one. The only thing I could find that might fill this requirement was a position selling cars. As I read through the want ads, I found a few places that offered a "free demo." That's where I began.

I got up early the next morning and caught a bus downtown to one of the dealerships advertising this "free demo." They sold Chryslers and Dodges, which weren't the most popular cars in those days, but that part didn't matter to me. It was all about getting the free car.

This particular company owned two huge car lots with Dodge on one side of the street and Chrysler on the other. My first interview was with a guy named Mick Saluzo. He was a decent enough guy, but not very encouraging when it came to my future with the company. I did, however, get past that first interview and ended up talking with the general manager, Ricco Pinzler. Ricco was one of the toughest guys I'd ever seen. He was kind of short and stocky but not what you would call overweight. He talked quite loudly, which caused some to think he was an expert at everything, but to me he was just a loud talker.

Although I had been working different jobs since I was ten years old, I have to admit I wasn't adept at pursuing one. This entire interview process was not something I was used to. As a result of my newness, I had a tendency to believe everything they told me. Of course, that was one of my greatest areas of vulnerability throughout my life. I just believed people. So when Mick and Ricco said, "We'll get back to you," I really thought they would. I practically lived by the phone for those first few days, thinking they were going to call any minute. After about four days I started thinking perhaps they lost my number. So, I gave them a call. They gave me some kind of story about how they had a lot of applicants to go through and how they could only pick a few. Then they alluded to my lack of experience in sales. I said, "I understand what you are saying, but how am I going to get any experience at my age unless somebody gives me a chance?"

Well, they didn't say yes, but they didn't say no either. They seemed to be talking in circles for a moment, then ended with, "Check back with us in a few days."

And I did. I called back in two days, in three days, in four days; I think I finally wore them down. On the fourth day they said, "Okay, come on down and we'll give you a try."

I knew they felt like they were taking a risk because they kept asking me how old I was. I would tell them, "Twenty-one" and they would say, "That's hard to believe because you look like you're fifteen."

And then laugh.

But that didn't matter to me, because the goal had been achieved. I got a car. They had no idea who they were getting. I was about to become the worst salesman they had seen in the car business. Actually, I didn't *become* the worst; I was just naturally the worst.

A large part of the problem was that I didn't really care much about selling. I just wanted a job and a car. Since the job paid minimum wage plus commission, I figured I could survive on the minimum wage if I didn't sell anything. Of course, I didn't want to look like a loser, so I did give it my best shot. The bigger problem was that I didn't have a clue about what to do or how.

They started my training in the new car department on the Dodge side. They were trying out a new program that was supposed to make great salespeople out of anyone. They were more interested in a person's outward appearance than they were about sales experience. They hired six of us all at once and we were supposed to go through a "demonstration" of the cars.

"This is an ashtray."

"This is the automatic door lock."

"This is the horn."

It all seemed quite silly to me, but I went along with the program because of the free car.

The training class went on for about two weeks and I became bored with the whole thing. During our breaks, however, I would slip over to the used car side and talk to some of the old-timers in the business. They were somewhat of a rough looking bunch, but pretty funny, and they seemed to know what they were talking about.

First there was Hank, a large black man who

was about fifty-five years old, six-foot four with a big potbelly. He taxied airplanes for United at night and sold cars during the day. He had a wife and two girlfriends, and about every other day they would all show up at once and have a huge fight in the parking lot. Poor ol' Hank; he didn't have a chance when they dug in. One time I saw all three of them hitting him with their purses, screaming and cussing at the same time. He looked pathetic. They must have had twenty-five kids between them.

Then there was Jeff. Jeff was always "stylin'." This was back in the Afro-six-inch-platform-shoes days. Jeff always talked big about how this car thing was just temporary until he got his big break in the movies. Unfortunately he had been selling cars for over five years without an interview for the movies in sight. Aside from his big plans and no plan to accomplish them, he was a great guy.

Then there was Neal. He was the smartest and the quietest of the bunch. He never said much, but when he did his words had weight. He was like a wise older uncle to the others. One of the funniest things I remember about Neal is a harmless prank Jeff kept playing on him. Jeff would borrow his lighter and when Neal wasn't looking, he would turn the adjustment up to make the flame jump out about four inches. Neal was a pipe smoker and liked to lean back in his chair, plop his feet up on the desk, and light his pipe. Well, after he'd get his lighter back from Jeff, he'd lean back, plop his feet up, and click that lighter.

It would catch him off guard, and he'd almost fall out of his chair. More than once I saw his hair almost catch on fire. This was particularly funny to me because even with all of Neal's wisdom, he'd fall for this gag about three times a week.

Finally, there was Carl. Carl was very scary looking. He never smiled and he never took part in the antics of the other guys. He kept to himself and rarely spoke. He just sat behind his desk staring out the window, waiting for his turn at a customer. I thought to myself, *Now ol' Carl could hurt somebody*. He just had that look about him.

Well, as I said, I spent most of my spare time over on the used car side and these guys told me things like, "Listen, Gary, you don't want to sell cars on the new car side. You can't make any money over there."

"It's too competitive and all the prices are preset."

"Over here we can make up our own prices, our commissions are higher, and nobody messes with us."

"Over on the new car side it's stuffy, boring, and they'll bog you down with their silly rules."

"If you get the chance, see if you can get transferred over here."

I thought this all sounded good, but it was out of my control.

Finally our class finished the training program and the big bosses sat down with each of us to tell us which dealership we were going to be assigned to, Chrysler or Dodge. Two were assigned to

Chrysler and two to Dodge, and then to my surprise, two were assigned to the used car lot and I was one of them. It is somewhat funny now as I look back on that day because I thought I had been "picked" to go to the used car side on account of my sales ability. I found out later if they didn't think someone was worth keeping, they would send the new salesperson to the used car side with the idea that it would be degrading to him so he would quit. It worked for most, but not in my case. I thought I had been given a promotion. None of those bosses could figure me out because I was so happy and just kept thanking them. I was thinking, *This is great. I'm going to get to work with the guys I like and I'll make a lot more money too.*

However, things didn't turn out quite like I expected. It didn't take long for everyone to realize I was the worst car salesman ever. I actually set a record for the greatest number of days in a row with no sales. I went for over three months without getting even one deal. But, I didn't mind; I had a car.

Some of the guys couldn't figure out why I didn't get fired. The company was exceptionally skilled at firing non-producers. Yet when talk began to circulate about cutting someone, I'd always get overlooked. I even wondered why myself, though I wasn't about to bring it up.

One day it became clear. I overheard Mick, the used car manager, talking to Ricco, the general manager. "I know he's not selling anything, but he's a good kid. Besides, he's the only real help I get around here. He does whatever I ask him to do. He locks up the cars at night, runs errands for me, and cleans up the offices. He's just a great guy to have around. If I ask one of the other guys to help do something, they just ignore me or tell me to do it myself."

The other guys didn't like Mick. They knew that he and Ricco were best friends and the only reason Mick got to be the manager was because of that friendship. So they used every chance they could to degrade him. Down deep he wanted to fire every one of them, but he didn't have the authority. He knew if it hadn't been for Ricco, he wouldn't be a manager; he'd be a salesman just like the rest of us. Naturally, since I did whatever he asked, he developed a sense of favor towards me. He became determined to keep me employed. He even sold some cars himself and told me to sign the contract so that I'd get credit for the sale. At first I said I couldn't do it because it was dishonest. He told me it wasn't dishonest because he was my boss and if he wanted to give a deal away here and there, it was his prerogative. "So, Gary, just keep your trap shut and sign the paperwork."

I didn't take the time to analyze it; I just obeyed.

The car business in downtown Los Angeles, at least during the 1970s, attracted odd sorts of people as employees. Of course, this doesn't say much for me, but my caveat was that I was there for the free car. Perhaps "odd" is not a fair description. "Colorful" is probably more accurate.

Take Hank for example. His personal life not withstanding, he was very entertaining. His smile revealed a couple of teeth missing. His big frame and booming voice were intimidating, but if you got to know him, you'd see a very sweet "teddy-bearish" manner. Personally, I loved the guy.

One afternoon I had the privilege of watching Hank at his best. He was sitting in the office area and blurted out, "I'm going to sell the next customer that walks on this lot, no matter what."

I thought to myself, *Hmmm, now this ought to be amusing*.

Only fifteen minutes went by before they arrived—a nice couple in their mid-thirties. At first glance I would have said they weren't in the mood to purchase anything that day, but were engaging in a great hobby among many who stopped by our lot: "Just looking."

I noticed Hank go a little above and beyond his duty to encourage them to make a purchase. He stood back for a moment and watched them until it appeared that they found a car of interest. Hank walked up to them and said in his booming voice, "You folks don't need to look any further, this is the car for you."

He proceeded to almost pick the guy up and stuff him in the front seat. This didn't surprise me at all because I had seen him do it before. I found it funny because Hank was totally oblivious to the looks of fear that swept over the customers' faces. He started talking, and when his "selling" kicked in, nobody could get a word in edgewise.

After about ten minutes of telling this couple what a great buy the car was, the husband decided to look a little closer at the vehicle's details. He reached over to the passenger side and opened the glove box. As the door opened, it fell off its hinges onto the floor. The guy picked up the glove box door. "Hey, look at this, it's broke!"

At first Hank tried to blame it on the customer by saying he broke it and now he had to buy the whole car. The customer wasn't going to be a pushover so he said, "You're not going to pull that one on me. I didn't break it; it just fell off into my hands. What kind of junk are you trying to sell me anyway?"

Hank was great. He always had an answer. It wasn't necessarily a great answer, but nonetheless, he had an answer. He reached over, grabbed the glove box door out of the customer's hand, turned, flung it half-way across the parking lot, and said, "Aw, forget it, you don't need a stupid glove box door anyhow. Tell you what, I'll knock fifty bucks off the deal. Now come on over to my office and we'll write this up."

Hank pulled the man out of the car and practically carried him to the office, talking a mile a minute on how this was the smartest decision the man could ever make. The guy's wife followed behind. I stood in amazement as I watched them sign on the dotted line.

Hank was fascinating, but he wasn't in the

same league with Carl. Carl by far was the most interesting salesman, and not necessarily in a good way. There were things that concerned me about Carl. For one, he never drove one of the dealership's cars. He only drove his own car. Sometimes Carl would stop by on his day off to pick up his paycheck and he'd pull into the lot driving his brand-new gold Cadillac. And he was never alone. He would always have four or five girls in the car with him. They would be hanging out the windows or the sunroof, talking and laughing very loudly. Carl would often turn and yell at them to "shut up and get back in the car." What struck me as odd was they did not respond to him like Hank's wife and girlfriends responded. With Hank they yelled back. With Carl, they obeyed.

After one such scene, I decided to find out the truth about Carl, so I struck up a conversation with Jeff.

"What is up with Carl? He never drives a company car, he always seems mean…and where did he get all those girlfriends? He's so nasty to them. Why do they keep hanging around a guy like that?"

At first Jeff didn't say anything. He just stared at me. Finally he spoke up and said, "Come on, Gary, You're joking, right?"

"What do you mean?"

"You're not serious are you? You know the answers to your questions, you're just trying to be funny, right?"

"No, Jeff, I don't know what you are talking

about."

"Gary, he drives that car and has those women because he's a pimp."

"You're kidding!"

Suddenly I began to feel incredibly ridiculous for my naivety.

"Okay, Jeff, if he's a pimp, what is he doing working here?"

"It's his cover. He has to have a regular job as a cover."

"Do Mick and Ricco know about this?"

"Yes, Gary, everybody knows, well, except you, and now you know."

"Why do they let that go on?"

"They say it's none of their business what anybody does in their spare time as long as they sell some cars."

Life was not the same from that day on. I had never felt very good about being around Carl before, but now I felt even worse. It was almost beyond my ability to comprehend that there were people in the world like this. Slowly but surely I began to form some subconscious columns in my mind regarding people. There were those who were good people with good intentions and good hearts, and then there were those like Raymond and Carl, in a category all their own. They were dishonest, deceitful, and predators of the weak and unsuspecting.

A few weeks later I was put in an awkward situation: I had to close up with Carl. I had done this numerous times with the other guys, but this was my first time to be alone all evening with Carl. Since we had never talked much before—and due to this new information—I was not looking forward to it. I knew I could not get by just sitting in my office and ignoring him. Even as I thought about my predicament, Carl called out, "Hey, Skinner, come over here to my office. I want to talk to you."

I thought, *Great, just what I wanted to do.*

I walked into his office, had a seat, and decided to let the conversation unfold. He started talking to me like I'd never heard him talk before. He wasn't asking me a lot of questions, he just rambled on and on about himself. He told me about "his women," how he not only had women here, but also "stables" all over the U.S. After about thirty minutes of bragging about the different cities where he had these ladies, he finished by saying, "Oh, another thing, Skinner, I'm an undercover cop too."

I didn't believe him, but I didn't want to disrupt his flow of confessions, nor bring attention to myself by disagreeing. He must have suspected that I wasn't buying into this last declaration, so he reached into his pocket and pulled out a badge. Then he pulled out a gun and set it on the desk. I thought, *A big part of me is having difficulty swallowing this cop angle, but something's telling me this is not the time to make any accusations. How in the world could a guy be a pimp and a cop at the same time? Then again, this is L.A.*

I don't know much about guns, but I do know

this one was real. As the evening wore on he seemed to take a liking to me. I wasn't sure if this was good or bad; I was just hoping our shift would hurry up and get over so we could lock up and I could go home. Just before the night ended he blurted out, "You know, Skinner, I kind of like you. You seem like a real decent kid. In fact, I want to give you something. It's my home phone number."

He handed me a 3X5 card with his first name and phone number on it.

"You need to know this number is private. I don't give it out to anyone unless I trust them. I'm doing this because I trust you and I want you to know I'm here for you. If you ever have any trouble, you just give me a call. For twenty-five bucks I can make anybody disappear."

I almost fell over. I didn't know what to say. It was obviously a very nice gesture on his part, but this was not the kind of gift I wanted to receive. On the other hand, this was not the kind of guy I wanted to reject and have turn on me. So I looked Carl in the eye, keeping my tone serious, and said, "Thanks, Carl. You can trust me."

I couldn't wait to get out of there and tear that card up.

Chapter 8

On a Roll

In retrospect it is interesting for me to see how much environment and associations contribute to the molding of a person's life. We have all been warned at different times to be cautious of where we go, and whom we spend time with. We've all heard phrases like "the wrong crowd," "bad examples," or "destructive relationships." Unfortunately, some of us have not always heeded those warnings.

I did not become good friends with my coworkers. We never got together after hours to "hang out." My only contact with them was in the workplace, yet their outlooks on life and their philosophies toward honesty and integrity did make an impact on me, particularly in light of my age and newness to this "big city" culture. I had been raised in a small community in the Midwest, and things that were common in a city of millions were unheard of in a town of a few thousand. In many ways it was as if I were visiting a different country with different core values, especially in this cutthroat business of selling cars.

A few more weeks passed. I was still not selling and there began to linger in the air a sense of "Skinner, your days are numbered around here."

I remember quite vividly the day I heard my name called over the intercom.

"Gary Skinner, please report to the new car showroom."

That was it. That was the signal that somebody in the head office was unhappy with me. I'd seen it happen several times before with other salesmen. I sat in my office for a moment thinking about what to do. About thirty seconds later, Mick poked his head around the corner and said, "Skinner, they want to move you over to the new car side to see if you can sell something there."

What he was really saying was that the management was fed up with my lack of production, but they were willing to give me one more chance.

"They are thinking perhaps you will do better in new cars because you won't have to lie about the product. All the cars over there are brand-new, they have a warranty, and you won't have to feel bad selling people something that's going to fall apart in three months."

It was true. A large part of my inability to sell was my inability to lie. If I knew something was wrong with a car, I felt obligated to tell the customer. This would often blow the deal. Down deep I knew Mick and the others were right. If I were to have any chance at doing well in this business, it would have to be under the umbrella of honesty.

"Skinner, I hate to lose you, but for now it's

your only hope to keep your job," Mick said.

As much as I appreciated their desire to help me, I couldn't stand the thought of working over in new cars. It was stuffy and plastic. Everyone practically stood at attention with phony smiles.

"I don't mean this as any disrespect to you or the others, Mick, but I'm not going. It's horrible over there. I like working here with you."

"I appreciate that Skinner, but you've got no other choice. Just do as they say and maybe you can come back after you get a few sales under your belt."

"I can't Mick. I'm not going."

"Skinner, they'll fire you."

"Then I guess they'll just have to fire me. I'm not going."

It was probably very puzzling to Mick and the others when I rebelled like I did because they saw me as a pushover. They didn't realize that I didn't fear much of anyone and I was already an expert rebel. They hadn't seen this side of me because nothing had happened yet to stir it up. The problem with me in those days was in part due to my immaturity. There is nothing wrong with having some stamina and conviction in your heart, but it is important to be able to discern between inner strength and plain old rebellion. This was rebellion.

Mick left the lot and headed to the new car side and I thought it was just a matter of minutes before they canned me. To my surprise, however, nothing happened. So, I just went about my day as if nothing was wrong. About an hour later, Ricco, the general manager, stomped into my office and said, "Skinner, get out here and watch me sell a car. It's time somebody around here showed you how to sell something."

A young married couple had just pulled up, so I followed Ricco out to meet them. He looked at me with the meanest scowl I'd ever seen, then turned toward them with a sweet, sugary smile and an equally phony greeting. The couple looked at a 1970 Dodge Dart. They were very observant, and if I could have read their minds, I would have said they saw through the phoniness from the beginning. In fact, they almost walked off the lot a couple of times in the middle of one of Ricco's sappy speeches.

One of the trickiest parts of selling is knowing when to shut up and start closing the deal. I will give Ricco this: He did have a good sense of timing. He began the close by talking about price. He quoted them the full price as posted on the window—which I thought was a brave thing to do in light of the fact that it was an embarrassing thousand dollars over reasonability. They practically laughed out loud. They were not by any means stupid consumers.

So he began to whittle the price down and push them to make a commitment. They kept shaking their heads and he kept dropping the price. It became obvious this was a matter of pride, and Ricco was not going to let these people leave. Just when I thought he had lost the sale, he blurted out, "Okay, folks, I know you want this car and I want you to have it. Let me tell you what I'm going to do. If you'll take this car today, right now, I'll sell it to you for $500 below our cost."

This didn't make any sense. We were never allowed to sell anything less than $200 *above* cost, and even that was considered extreme. All of a sudden I realized this was to be a lesson of ridiculousness from Ricco to me, though I'm sure he didn't see it that way. He had to prove to me that he could sell at will.

They hesitated for a moment and then said, "Okay, we'll take it."

It took about an hour before the couple finished all the paperwork and drove off the lot, but as soon as they did, Ricco walked into my office and said, "Now Skinner, *that's* how to sell a car."

I couldn't have been more insulted. I looked at him with the most innocent look I could muster and said in the most respectful tone I could, "Thanks for the lesson Mr. Pinzler. I didn't realize we could sell our cars for $500 under cost."

It wasn't the smartest thing I could have said, and definitely not the most respectful. His face turned red and he became so angry that if Carl's gun had been handy, I think he would have shot me. Instead, he turned on his heels and stormed out the door. I assumed that I was fired now. But there was one problem for Ricco: All of this happened in front of the other guys. So he decided to cut his losses and go back to his office to cool down.

It was very quiet for a few minutes. Nobody really knew what to say. Mick rolled his eyes at me and ran after Ricco, probably to keep him from finding a baseball bat. It all happened so fast I didn't know what to do except sit there. Suddenly Jeff blurted out, "Skinner, You're full of surprises. I didn't know you had it in you to stand up to ol' Ricco like that."

The next thing I knew, the whole room roared with laughter and everybody patted me on the back. This may sound like a happy ending, but the truth is, I didn't feel good about myself for how I had disrespected my boss, even if he was an unreasonable cuss sometimes.

As much as I expected it, I did not get fired. In fact, Ricco started being a lot nicer to me, which was puzzling. Perhaps he realized he wasn't being fair with me, or maybe he noticed I was maturing some. He had viewed me as a kid who couldn't sell, but perhaps I had grown up a little, at least in his eyes. This did not negate the fact that I was wrong to speak to him like I did.

About three weeks after the "sales lesson" from Ricco, the inevitable happened.

"Gary Skinner, report to Mr. Pinzler's office immediately."

I knew exactly what that meant. Everybody knew. It was curtains for ol' Gary. I knew this would not be a pretty scene. I had been expecting this day for over six months. I thought, *I might as well get it over with so I can move on with my life.*

I will admit that I didn't look forward to the confrontation.

Ricco's office overlooked the new car showroom and there must have been at least thirty steps to the top. The stairs were inside the showroom so everybody working in that area sat there watching; yet pretending to not pay attention to whomever was taking the trip. The fact is, as soon as Pinzler's office door shut, everybody started gossiping like crazy. I didn't witness this as much as those who worked in new cars, but I'd been in there for a couple of those events. The rumor was that everybody who walked up those stairs to see Ricco walked back down either shaking all over or crying or both. I could never figure out why it had to be done this way. I thought, *Why can't these matters be handled more pleasantly? What is the purpose of humiliation?*

Of course, I knew the answer. Ricco and some of the others had fun talking about the incident later in the day. They all seemed to get a big kick out of making a grown man cry.

Today would be a little disappointing for Ricco, because I didn't plan on crying. In fact, I thought about telling him to come on down to the showroom floor and fire me there. Thirty steps was a lot of work.

I walked into the showroom and sure enough, everyone pretended to be busy with something else. I found it comical. I walked up the stairs and knocked on Ricco's door.

"Come on in Skinner."

I walked in, and he was standing right there. He closed the door and began his diatribe. It was nasty. He didn't just talk, he yelled. I had never heard so many cuss words in one setting before in my life. He called me everything in the book and finished every sentence with "lousiest salesman in the world."

He must have turned three or four different colors during his rampage. I thought a couple of times he was going to have a stroke or a heart attack. Finally, he stopped. It seemed like he had ranted for about twenty minutes, but it was probably more like five. I didn't have a clue what to do except stand there and listen. I didn't especially appreciate all the negative things he was saying, but I figured he would wear himself out eventually. Obviously, his vocabulary was limited. About half way through his craziness I thought, *Aside from all this cussing and meanness, this is kind of entertaining*.

I stood toe to toe with him, remaining calm, not saying a word. He finally ran out of steam, walked over to his chair behind his desk, and plopped down.

"So, Skinner, are you just going to stand there? Don't you have anything to say for yourself?"

"Well, Mr. Pinzler, as a matter of fact I do. As I was standing here listening to you, I couldn't help but think you were right. I really haven't done a good job for you around here, and to tell you the truth, I hate that I've let you down. Let's face it, you've been more than fair with me, and before I leave here today I want you to know how much I appreciate all the patience you've shown me."

His demeanor began to change as I continued, "If I were you, I would have fired me a long time ago. You know, as I think of it, you're a pretty fair guy. I hate that I'm getting fired, but I want you to know that I've learned a lot while I've been here. I believe that wherever I go, I can look back and say that I'm a better man for working here with you."

I walked over to his desk, put my hand out, and waited for him to shake it. He just looked at it. He kept staring at my hand, then back at my face, with a look of total perplexity. He finally broke the silence. "Sit down, Skinner. Listen, I didn't mean to fly off at you like I did. You're a decent guy and you don't deserve to get yelled at like that, even if you are a lousy salesman. And let's face it, you really are lousy."

"Yeah, I know. But while you were telling me how lousy I am, I got an idea. I was thinking that I bet I know what my problem has been. I'm not any good at selling used cars because it seems like there is so much lying involved to get them sold. I bet if I had an opportunity to sell new cars, I could do it."

He just stared at me for a moment looking like he was going to blow up all over again.

"We already tried that Skinner. Remember, we tried to get you to come over to the new car side, but you were too stubborn to make the change."

"Yeah, I know, that was really poor judgment on my part."

"Listen, Skinner, it's too late. You blew your chance."

"I understand. You're absolutely right. I blew it."

"It's not that I still wouldn't give you a chance, but we're over staffed as it is and somebody has got to go, and you're it."

"No problem, Mr. Pinzler, once again, thanks for the opportunity you've given me."

He sat there for another couple of minutes staring at the wall in silence. Then he said, "Aaaaah, I can't believe I'm doing this. I don't have any room here, but maybe Mr. Lawson has some space across the street at the Chrysler lot. Sit tight while I give him a call."

He pressed a speed dial button on his phone and Mr. Lawson answered, "Lawson here."

"Hey Lawson, this is Pinzler, I'm sitting here in my office with Skinner. I've got my speaker-phone on so he can hear everything we're saying. I just finished telling him what a lousy salesman he is. He says he needs to sell new cars instead of used. I told him we don't have any room for him over here, but that I'd check to see if you had any space over there. Just tell me what you want to do. If you don't have any room, or even if you don't want the headache of a lousy salesman on your staff, I'll send him on his way."

"No, don't do that. Send him on over. We'll give him a try."

I couldn't believe it. They didn't fire me. That was insane. I couldn't sell their rotten lousy lemon cars for more than eight months and here I'd just sold the toughest customer in the company, the general manager, on me, a rotten lousy lemon of a salesman. Now that's funny. To top it all off, he opened the door for me to leave his office, put his arm around me, and walked me all the way down the stairs, smiling, as if we were best friends. This must have really fouled up the gossip. The employees in the showroom probably had a pool going and more than likely somebody lost some serious change that day betting against me.

I walked back to my desk in used cars and told the guys what happened. They all got a big chuckle out of the story and kept shaking their heads as I walked across the street.

I worked for Mr. Lawson for about two weeks and still didn't sell anything. He ended up trading me back to the Dodge store in exchange for someone else. There I was, right back where I started, except now I was on the new car side of Dodge.

The manager of new cars was a man named Jim Leonard. He was about the nicest and most patient person I'd ever met. In fact, I couldn't figure out why he was working for a company like this. There was nothing about his personality that fit with the other managers. We hit it off right away. He didn't talk about my past failures, he just asked me one thing. "Gary, has anyone tried to teach you how to sell?"

I said, "Well, I'm sure they have, but for whatever reason it hasn't worked."

"Will you do me a favor? Will you trust me and do whatever I tell you to do?"

"Sure, as long as it's not dishonest."

So he sat me down and began to teach me. He taught me how to talk to the customers, how to listen to what they were saying, and how to help them get what they wanted. I started selling within a couple of days. In fact, I sold eight cars in three days. Everyone was beside themselves. They couldn't believe it. To be honest, I couldn't believe it either.

Within a week, however, I started to get bored with selling cars, so I quit. I decided to take a job selling auto parts over the phone. Big mistake. I did even worse.

This is how things work when you're under a curse. You make ridiculous, irrational decisions based upon nothing. You live by whims. You stop seeing the big picture, and you continue being sloppy in your thinking, sloppy in your living, and sloppy in your judgments. My moving to Los Angeles was foolish, my taking the car sales job was foolish, my idea of selling auto parts over the phone was foolish, and now I was about to top off all this foolishness with the mistake of all mistakes.

Chapter 9

Out of Control

One of the most difficult things to do when telling a true story is to include key components that are not very flattering to the characters involved. I find this especially troublesome. To help myself in writing this and to help you in reading, it is imperative to understand an important concept. People are the way they are for a reason. We are all a product of our environment, our up bringing, and our culture. This is not meant to excuse behavior but to give some perspective. I believe we are all given opportunities to respond positively or negatively to our circumstances. History books are filled with names of those who were extremes on either side. With this in mind I will endeavor to be as kind and honest as possible in retelling this next difficult, but very real part of my life.

We met at the car dealership. We had both been hired to work in sales. She was beautiful, intelligent, cunning, and sensuous. She was from Sweden. She was incredibly intimidating and had an uncanny way of manipulating me into doing just about anything for her. This may sound like I was somewhat of a victim, but I was a very willing victim.

A huge problem for me was that love and lust were completely twisted in my mind. I was twenty-two years old, my hormones were in high gear, and the next thing I knew, I was engaged. I don't remember how it happened. As silly as it sounds, I can't remember if I asked her or if she asked me, or if she just told me we were. It was by far the most surreal time of my life.

Reva had an extremely sad story. I was always a sucker for a sad story, especially if the main character was beautiful. I could not imagine how anyone could have survived all that she had been through. I thought, *No wonder she struggles with anger and bitterness. The poor girl has never been given a fair chance.*

So from the beginning our relationship was founded on lust and pity, a poor combination. Though Reva said she believed in God, she was not what I considered an example of Christianity, at least by the standards of my upbringing. But who was I to judge? I wasn't much of an example those days myself. Nothing I did in the present was representative of Christ. The only link I kept with my faith was attending church and occasionally praying.

I knew I had allowed my emotions and my physical attraction to Reva to get the better of me. I knew I was doing the wrong thing and I needed to stop, break off the relationship, and get my life right with God. It's pathetic to admit, but I just couldn't seem to find the strength. As the relationship continued Reva became more and more bold in articulating her motives for marrying me. She would say at times, "You know, Gary, I'm not sure I even love you. The main reason I'm interested in you is if you marry me, I can get a green card. I'm an illegal alien."

She would laugh and say, "Of course I'm kidding, darling, I'm crazy about you."

Then she would start kissing me and the next thing I knew, I was in love all over again.

Other times when we were together, I would go into an exceptionally strong mode and become determined to call it off.

"This isn't going to work. I can't marry you."

Reva would withdraw from me, begin sobbing, and say, "I can't believe you would hurt me so much. You are just like all the other men who wanted to use me and hurt me. You're no different. All I've ever had is pain and here you are giving me more. Just get out of my life."

"I'm sorry, I don't want to cause you more pain. I just don't see how this can work."

"Of course you can't, you are just a little boy. If you were a man you would know how to love me. Oh, well, I'm probably unlovable. You need to go find yourself some little girl from your grade school and marry her. You aren't ready to handle a real woman. You're just a weak little boy. Now get away from me and leave me to my crying, I've had enough pain in my life without you hurting me more."

"Please, don't say that. I am not trying to hurt

you."

"Then what is wrong with me? Am I ugly?"

"Of course you're not ugly."

"I know, you can't handle my past. You can't love someone as unlovable as me. I hear you talk about Jesus and His love, but it doesn't sound like you have that kind of love."

"Yes I do. I can love you. You are not unlovable."

Then through almost uncontrollable sobs she would say, "Yes, I am and I don't blame you for not wanting me."

"But you're wrong, I do want you, I do care about you. I don't want to hurt you."

"Then why are you hurting me?"

"I'm sorry."

After that she would move over close and begin to lightly kiss me and ask me to hold her. Next thing I knew, I was in love all over again. It was a terrible cycle.

The strange part was if I were away from her for a couple of days, I would come to my senses and realize the relationship was a disaster, with no redeeming value. She wised up to this and began to almost never let me out of her sight. She expected me to spend every moment with her that I wasn't working. If I said, "I can't stop over tonight, so I'll see you tomorrow," she would call me just before I got off work.

"Oh, Gary, please. You don't need to stay long, but I fixed you a wonderful dinner. I worked on it all afternoon. Please stop by and have supper with me. You have to eat something. Please, just have dinner with me, then you can go."

"No, I really can't come by tonight."

"Oh, Gary, please come and see what I prepared for you."

"All right, I'll stop by in about an hour and a half, but I can't stay long."

"That's fine, I'll see you then."

Unfortunately for me, she was not an average cook. In fact, I couldn't believe how gifted she was in the culinary arts. So I would stop by, remind her that I couldn't stay long, sit down to a fine meal, and the next thing I knew, I was in love all over again. I was hopeless.

To make things worse, she started going to church with me. She got to me from every angle: the "below the belt" angle, the "stomach" angle, the "pleasing to the eyes" angle, and now the "heart" angle. I realize this might sound cynical, but it really isn't. I mentioned earlier how Raymond and Carl were predators. Now I was about to marry one. Of course I didn't see Reva as a predator. To me she was a beautiful woman who had lots of talents and someone who I could make happy. I thought I was her only chance in life. She had been through so much hurt and pain, and I just knew that I would never hurt her. It wasn't in me to do so.

The church we attended had the nicest pastor you would ever want to meet. I told her we couldn't get married unless we went through premarital counseling. This poor guy didn't have a chance. Nothing against him, but he just was not up to the task. He really did try to help us make the right decision, but by the second or third meeting, she moved in for the kill. I don't think he fully trusted her, but he did trust me, so when he asked, "Gary, are you sure she's the right one?" I answered, "Yes, of course I'm sure," knowing I wasn't sure about anything. I hoped I was right.

Moreover, Reva always had an explanation as to why things were the way they were. She was an illegal alien because after she came to America on a three-month visa, she was afraid to go back to Sweden. I can't remember if she said her life was in danger or what, but she wanted to stay in America and all would be fine if she could just get her green card. I didn't know anything about her parents except she was adopted and had not seen them in years, and there had been some problems. She had a daughter, Shannon, who was currently staying with a wonderful family in the area: an older couple who served as foster parents to several kids. In fact, we visited her a couple of times and wanted her to live with us as soon as we were married.

I would like to say the entire relationship blind-sided me, but in reality, I was given plenty of warnings.

My parents, who had never met Reva, warned me, "Gary, you are making a terrible mistake."

Reva told me, "Your parents are being over protective. They don't want their little boy to grow up and get married. They want to keep you tied to their apron strings. They are being selfish. Nobody will ever be good enough for their little Gary."

My friend Archie shared his concerns.

She said, "Of course he doesn't want you to get married, he'll be stuck with the rent by himself. You are taking care of him and he knows it. Besides, he's probably just jealous and lonely himself."

The family who was taking care of Shannon warned me.

Reva said, "You can't trust that family. They are a nice couple, but down deep they want to take Shannon away from me. They are grandparents and they make a lot of money from the state by taking care of her, so if we get married and take her with us, they'll be out the money."

The guys at work warned me, even Carl the pimp. Isn't that funny—the pimp had better discernment than I did.

Reva reasoned, "How can you possibly trust a bunch of used car salesmen? Especially Carl. Why he's a pimp. How could you listen to the advice of a pimp?"

All of these explanations were very weak. My parents were not opposed to me marrying, they just wanted to meet my fiancée. But she knew if they did, that that would be the end. Archie wasn't worried about the rent; he was just trying to look out for me. The family taking care of Shannon was already well off financially. They loved Shannon and wanted the best for her. As far as Carl was concerned, he had no stakes in this at all. There was nothing for him to gain if I did or did not get married.

I didn't listen. I was a fool.

I'll never forget the day of our wedding. My parents were not there because Reva insisted we change the wedding date, and for the life of me I can't remember why except that she always got her way. I stood in the front of the church next to the pastor and she stood at the end of the aisle, ready to walk toward me. Just as the music began to play, in an almost audible voice, I heard God speak to my heart.

"Gary, stop. Do not go through with this. Do not marry her."

"But Lord, it's too late. Besides, she needs me. I can help her."

"Gary, turn around and walk out. It's not too late."

"I know it's going to be tough at times, but I can handle it. I'll make it work. You'll see. She needs me. I can help her change."

By then Reva was halfway down the aisle, and the voice left. I thought, *Maybe that wasn't God. I haven't exactly been an obedient follower lately, so why would He talk to me? These are just thoughts that come with last minute jitters.* .

Within twenty-four hours, I knew it was Him.

The next few months became even more scattered and confusing than the ones leading up to the wedding. Now it was official; I was married. I had prepared my mind for some pitfalls and mood swings that might occur from time to time, but I was in no manner prepared to handle this relationship.

Not long after our "I do's" I dreaded coming home. From the moment I walked in the door till I went to bed, I was faced with a barrage of demands and false accusations. A typical evening would begin with, "So where have you been? I thought you were coming straight home from work."

"I did."

"Well, you're late. I had supper ready ten minutes ago and now it's ruined."

"You know how traffic is around here. We can't plan dinner to be at a precise moment with the possibilities of unforeseen delays."

"That's no excuse. I'm sure you were goofing off somewhere or you stopped to see someone along the way."

"That's not true, I came straight home."

"Well, you better have, because I'm not going to put up with a husband who doesn't respect me."

"What?"

"You heard me. Now get over there and wash the dishes. I'm not going to slave all day at work, then come home and wait on you hand and foot. I'm not a maid service you know."

"I never said you were. Why are you talking to me like this?"

"Let's face it Gary, you just can't take care of me. You're not doing a very good job as a husband or provider."

"Give me a break, we've only been married a few days. I'll do better. I'll help out around the house. I don't expect you to do everything."

After about twenty or thirty minutes of bantering back and forth like this I would wash the dishes and clean the kitchen and do just about anything she demanded to keep her calm. Often I spent the rest of the evening sitting on the front steps or walking around outside talking to myself about what a mess I'd gotten myself into. I tried praying, but I didn't have any confidence that God was paying attention to me.

After about three weeks, I thought about becoming Catholic to see if I could get an annulment. I didn't know the rules, but I was desperate. Since I didn't believe in divorce under any circumstances, I thought about leaving her, remaining married, but living in peace alone. I was pondering this at work when the phone rang.

"Gary, guess what? I'm pregnant."

"You're what?"

"I'm pregnant."

"You've got to be kidding."

I was stunned because there had been a huge shortage of intimacy between us. I had never heard of anyone getting pregnant without sex.

I drove home early that day with a lot of questions and mixed feelings. A huge part of me was actually excited about being a dad. Another part of me was scared to death. I didn't know how to react to Reva. This was a typical dilemma because she was so difficult to predict. It was impossible to be myself because that always brought down a wrathful response. As I drove home I rehearsed my options. If I acted disappointed, she would be angry and claim I didn't want to have any children with her. If I acted happy and excited, she would rail on me for what I'd "done to her," and how she had to suffer all the pain and difficulty of a pregnancy. If I acted indifferent, she would lecture me on my immaturity and selfishness. I decided to go with "happy and excited." In retrospect, it was the right choice, but her response was still very frustrating. I couldn't win.

I listened to her endless complaining that evening with an inner hope that maybe, just maybe this baby would bring something good to our relationship. Over the course of the next week Reva became even more unpredictable with her moods and expectations. At times I actually thought I was losing my mind. Aside from all my other poor decisions, I knew anger was never the right response, so in many respects what happened next was very much out of character for me.

I walked in the house from work. Reva was in the bedroom. I went in to check on her and she began another one of her seemingly endless lectures about us, the baby, our finances, her pain, the heat, our future, her disappointment in me, and on and on and on. During this string of blabbering she uttered the words, "I've decided to have an abortion."

I woke up from my mental slumber, got about six inches from her face, pointed my finger, and said in a loud tone that left no room for discussion, "You will NOT murder our baby. I can tolerate just about anything, but I will not tolerate this kind of talk or this kind of thinking. Just get it out of your head. Abortion is not an option."

I felt the heat in my face. I didn't give her an ultimatum. I didn't have to. She knew she'd stepped over the line. The good news is she never ever brought it up again.

I don't recall exactly when the decision was made, but soon after I called my parents and told them I wasn't making it financially. They were very gracious and offered me a job with my dad's business. I accepted. I told Reva the plan and for some reason, she didn't give me any guff about it. She actually agreed it was a good idea. So we headed back to the Midwest to start our family. Before we left California, however, we needed to make a very important decision.

"What about Shannon?"

Apparently, Reva had been talking to the foster family and they were discussing the possibilities of her moving with us. It seemed like a no-brainer to me. Shannon was Reva's, so of course she would come with us. But I didn't realize it wasn't that cut and dry.

Shannon had not lived with her mother for any length of time during her six years of life. In a way, she was in a lot more stable circumstance with her temporary family than she would be with us. Unfortunately Shannon was put in the difficult place of making a choice between being with her mother and I, or staying with the foster family. This was an unfair position to put any child in, but nonetheless, it was what took place. Shannon did the best she knew at such a young age and chose us. We packed up our few belongings and flew home to Indiana. I became an instant dad.

Chapter 10

A Not So Merry Go-Round

Returning home to Indiana was filled with a lot of mixed emotions. I was hugely relieved because I knew at the very least, my parents wouldn't let use starve. I was also embarrassed. I'd made a mess of my life. Yet I was determined to make the best of it.

Over the next few months several things happened, some good, some not so good. One of the good things—and perhaps the wisest decision I made during those troublesome days—was the commitment to be the greatest dad I could for both the baby on the way and Shannon. I didn't waste any time in making the necessary arrangements to adopt her. If she was going to be stuck with us, she needed to be completely with us, and in particular, she needed something she had never known before: a real dad. By the time the baby arrived Shannon was in full swing as my daughter, Reva had received her green card, and finally, I thought, life had a semblance of normalcy.

I tried to bring to our home the same values my parents had brought to my sister and I growing up, like going to church, having meals together as a family, providing an atmosphere of love and peace around the house. It became an uphill battle on every front.

My wife attended church seasonally, but I never knew what inspired a particular season to start or end. Such was the case with everything. Her entire life seemed like a house of mirrors and it was impossible to determine what was real, including her temperament. One moment Reva could be delightful, funny, and downright enjoyable to be around. The next moment, without warning, she spewed anger and made unreasonable demands. No matter how much I tried, I never got used to this volatile lifestyle. I often gave into Reva's demands in order to keep the peace and provide some sense of stability for Shannon and Todd.

Probably the best thing that happened to Shannon and Todd during those days was Grandma and Grandpa. They were very committed to making life good for the kids. I have no idea what I would have done without them, especially in the years to come, because, yes, life became worse.

Aside from the continuous arguing, new challenges arose, specifically, financial. Although we weren't living a great lifestyle, we were living within our means and I hoped things would improve. About a year after Todd was born, my wife decided she wanted to go back to work. She chose to sell expensive vacuum cleaners.

Of course, Reva didn't want to be known as a

vacuum cleaner salesperson, so she made great efforts to camouflage what the product really was. Aside from this charade, vacuums were dependable and Reva became quite skilled at selling them.

For a while, things got better. Reva wasn't home much, so we couldn't argue. She earned decent money and bought herself lots of new clothes. This seemed to make her very happy. (The only downside was her rule: The money I made was "our" money; the money she made was "her" money.)

Our little Todd developed more and more each day, and Shannon did well in school. We stayed in contact with the foster family in California and Shannon visited them some in the summers.

Over the course of the next few years, I quit my job with my dad's business and got involved in selling vacuums. Reva and I tried working together as a team. That didn't work. Then we each operated our own separate businesses. That didn't work. We began a cycle of moving from one town to another, starting a business, closing the business, and starting again.

Somewhere in the midst of this Reva began to disappear for two and three weeks at a time. She went to Las Vegas or Atlantic City to "get away" because she "needed a break." She would call and say she won a bundle, then a few hours later call again to say she lost it all. On one occasion a casino called to tell me she bounced a check for $3,000. Once again, life was not good.

After we had been married for about six years,

some new developments began to unfold. Shannon was now fourteen and had grown up to be quite a beautiful girl. She obviously had inherited much of the "beauty" traits of her mother, but unfortunately, she had inherited some of her temperament as well. More than once I had to take some drastic measures to break the two of them up from bitter arguments and screaming contests. What was about to happen did not totally surprise me, but at the same time I didn't want to believe it.

I came home one day to one of those screaming matches with threats being thrown on both sides. Her mom finally went upstairs and Shannon came to me in tears. "Dad, I need you to go downtown and sign some papers that will allow me to become a ward of the state so I can live with another family."

"No, Shannon, I can't do that. I know things are bad, but we need to work it out."

"No, Dad, you don't understand. Things between Mom and I are worse than you know. I can't live here anymore. I can't live with her anymore. Dad, if I don't leave, I'm afraid something terrible is going to happen. Either Mom is going to kill me, or I'm going to kill her."

That shook me up. As I looked at Shannon, I knew her fear was not contrived; it was real. I also had seen moments where they both looked like they were capable of taking the other out. I agreed to Shannon's request. That day became one of the saddest of my life.

"Listen, Dad, I'm still going to live in the area.

You and Todd can come visit me. You're still my dad, and I still love you. I just can't live like this anymore."

So Shannon was gone, off to another family. Actually off to several families before she found a place that proved safe. I tried to stay in contact with her, but she seemed to drift further and further away from me. I wanted to stay close, but there were so many fires to put out in my own life. She grew up fast. She learned how to manage without me. Time, location, and circumstances seemed to keep us apart. I failed her as a father.

Although Todd and I did not have to hear anymore of those fights between mother and daughter, life at home did not improve. The anger and bitterness seemed to turn toward us. Todd and I were close, very close. We did everything together. Consequently, whenever his mom and I argued, Todd automatically clung to me. Reva's response in those moments were to storm out of the house and leave us standing there, or to say, "Get out of this house, and take your boy with you."

During those years Todd found ways to escape mentally. He was only six but he developed two passions: baseball and reading. I have never seen anybody read as many books as he did. I couldn't keep enough of them around. As a result, it often felt like I was having conversations with a little man rather than a little boy. He could talk sports with the adults and keep them on their toes. Yet he was still a little boy and some of the junk he saw and heard in our house was definitely not healthy.

He always seemed to arrive at some interesting perspectives. I remember once when he and I were coming back from visiting Shannon. He asked, "Dad, do we have to go home? Why can't we live with Shannon's new family?"

When he said that, it began to sink in just how bad things had become for him. Somehow I thought since he was so young, he wasn't aware of the severity of our circumstances.

The time had come for some drastic changes. Actually they were way overdue. Shannon had left, my son was afraid to be home without me, and their mom was back to her old habits of gambling and whatever else. We had started marriage counseling at a local church, but she refused to go again after the second meeting.

I told her, "Something has to change. I'm not going to live like this any longer. I'm going away for a week to get my thoughts together and when I come back, I'm moving out until we get some counseling and I see some improvement."

I was not planning on getting a divorce. I was just going to change my address and live separately from her. This was no life for me and Todd or anyone else for that matter. It was time for me to take a stand against this persistent irrational behavior. Talking and hoping had not facilitated any changes to date; action was the only recourse. I thought, *Perhaps this is what it is going to take to get Reva's attention*.

At the end of that week, I walked in the door and she handed me the papers. She had filed for divorce. Reva had also taken another step that I never considered a possibility. She filed for sole custody of Todd. She told him I was leaving and he was staying with her. The terror in his eyes said it all.

I couldn't believe my ears. This made absolutely no sense whatsoever. Why in the world would Reva make such a drastic move when she never spent any time with him up to this point? I realize in some strange way she was trying to get even with me.

I walked away that day absolutely devastated. I knew right away I would need a good attorney because Reva was going to play hardball. I don't remember how I found the guy I did, but I do remember my request. "I don't care about anything except Todd. She can have everything else."

I gave my attorney the details of our situation hoping he would have some good news regarding custody. He said it was almost unheard of for the father to be awarded the children in a divorce. He suggested I push to get the best deal I could on visitation and live with it. This was almost more than I could handle. It wasn't right, but I had no choice. I had to make the best of the lousy terms. He negotiated for me to be able to have Todd every other weekend while we were in the divorce process.

Every other week on Friday afternoon I'd pick Todd up and bring him back on Sunday evening. He was always ready and waiting when I arrived. After a few visits I found out he was actually ready, waiting by the door with his little suitcase at least an hour ahead of time. I would pull up to the driveway and he would run out to the car, open the door, throw his stuff in the backseat, and practically be sitting on my lap. Then he'd say, "Come on Dad, let's get out of here" as if we were escaping.

His mom would look out the window or stand in the doorway and I would wave. Then I'd tell Todd to wave good-bye. He would wave and then say, "Ok, Dad, that's enough, let's get out of here."

Those weekends were very hard work from a discipline perspective. Todd was so unruly it was embarrassing. We would stop at a fast food place and while I was at the counter placing our order, he would run around the room, turning over chairs, throwing napkins in the air, and stuffing his pockets with ketchup packets. More than once I had to stop ordering and chase him down. I'd grab his shirt, pick him up in the air, and make it very clear this was not going to work with me around. These weekends were very special to me, but difficult because I had to spend ninety percent of the time disciplining him. I was beginning to get concerned that he would begin to resent me. What I found, however, was just the opposite. He wanted all the more to be with me.

The worst part was when it was time to take Todd back to his mom. He would ask me, "Dad, why do I have to go back? Why can't I stay with you?"

I would try my best to explain it, but it never

seemed to be a good enough answer for him or me. We would pull into the driveway, and then it would happen. I would take him by his little hand and walk to the door with him crying uncontrollably and begging me to not make him stay there. She would come to the door, take his hand, and pull him inside. He would be crying and begging, right in front of her. "Please, Dad, don't leave me here. Please don't make me stay with her. Please, don't leave me."

She would pull him inside and shut the door in my face.

This went on for over three months. Then I saw him learning how to deal with it. He stopped crying about leaving me and stopped saying how much he didn't want to be with her. But there was something different about his demeanor. He was forced to grow up much too soon. He stopped reacting with his heart and began managing with his head. Since he was quite intelligent, his brain won.

Finally, at the end of eight months, we got a break.

I came to pick Todd up one day and Reva met me at the door and asked, "Gary, how would you like to keep Todd for the summer?"

That was an easy question. We packed up his gear and drove to my parent's house. While I worked through the divorce, I stayed with my parents. Nothing could have been better for Todd. He loved his grandma and grandpa, and between the three of us, we were able to get past the discipline issue. He just needed some consistency.

Within a few days he settled down.

It was a great summer. Halfway through I got a call from my attorney. He said we had a court date to finalize everything and I needed to bring Todd to the courthouse to wrap things up. About forty-five minutes after we got there, they called us in. The only people in the courtroom were the judge, a stenographer, my attorney, Todd, and myself. Mom didn't show up. I thought to myself, *This is too good to be true. After all the squabbling and arguing about where Todd should live, she doesn't even show up to make her case.*

The judge asked where the mom was and since nobody knew, he proceeded to go ahead with the process. He asked Todd where he would prefer to live. "With Dad."

The judge declared everything final and gave me custody of my son. We both cried with joy when we got in the car that day. Everything was going to be okay.

Later that night I got a call from Reva. "Gary, I found out today that the court gave you custody of Todd, but I hope you will still allow him to see his mother from time to time."

"Of, course I will. I have no intention of keeping him from you."

"I'm glad to hear that. I was thinking I would drive up to where you live this Sunday and take him to the mall, and maybe a movie and dinner. Would that be okay with you?"

"Sure, that would be fine."

Sunday rolled around. Todd's mom stopped by and the two of them went to the mall. All day before she arrived, Todd kept asking me, "Are you sure it will be okay for me to be with Mom? I will get to come back home today, won't I? Why do I have to go with her?"

"Todd, you need to go with her because she is your mom. I promise you, the whole thing will go by quickly. You'll go to the mall, she'll probably buy you some toys, you'll get to eat at any restaurant you want, you'll go to a movie, and then you'll be back here with us. It will be a good time. Don't worry."

I have to admit I was not happy about it either, but I convinced myself her request was by no means unreasonable and she deserved to have him just as much as I did. She was his mom.

I didn't become concerned until about 8:30 PM. The mall closed at 8:00, but I thought, *They probably got a late start on one of the movies and they'll be home any time now*.

Then it was 9:00, then 9:30, then 10:00, then 10:30. By now I was more than a little anxious. Finally the phone rang.

"Gary, I wanted you to know that Todd is safe. He is with me. You know, your attorney did something illegal. He didn't notify me of the court date. That's why I wasn't there, and I want you to know the paperwork you have is not worth anything. I have new paperwork and mine says Todd gets to stay with me until we have another court date. You thought you were pulling a fast one on me, but it didn't work. I've got Todd and he's staying with me."

Click.

I stood there for a moment in utter disbelief.

What was she talking about? I have the paperwork, signed by a judge, that says Todd stays with me. How could this have happened?

All I could think about was Todd. *The poor little guy thought he was just going to the mall and then back home. He is probably confused and scared.*

My dad and I drove to the police station and told them what happened. They said there was nothing I could do. The next day we drove to Reva's town and went to the school she had put Todd in. When I arrived, the teacher told me I couldn't see my son and if I didn't leave the property immediately, she would call the police and have me arrested.

"What? That's crazy! I'm his dad, I have the right to see my own son whenever I want."

She said his mom had warned them that if I showed up and caused any problem, to call the police. She had a court order.

My dad had to practically drag me out of that building. He finally got me to the car and tried calming me down. There was nothing else I could do for the moment, so we drove home. I called my attorney but he was "busy." In fact, he never did return my calls. The consensus was I needed to get a new attorney and start over. Obviously the guy I had was a bit on the shady side.

Over the next couple of days I found a new

attorney and explained what happened. He just shook his head and sighed. He was very cut and dry about his advice, and though he was a little more expensive, at least I felt like he would do things legally.

Once he was on the case he was able to negotiate for me to have Todd again on the weekends. This went on for another couple of months before a new court date was set. My attorney did not paint a pretty picture, and in fact, said I should get used to the fact that I would only see Todd a couple of times each month.

About a week before the court date, I was walking around in the yard, talking to God and saying, "Lord, if this is the way it has to be, I ask that you protect Todd's heart and show me how to be the best dad I can with the little time I get to have with him. Lord, I trust You. I know You are watching over him."

All of a sudden an indescribable peace came over me and I had this thought, *Todd is going to live with me permanently. I don't know how it's going to work out, but I just know he's going to be with me. Either the judge will rule in my favor or Reva will just give him up.*

Our final court date was scheduled on a Wednesday. It was now the Sunday prior. Todd had been with me for the weekend and I needed to take him back to his mother. When we arrived in her town, we realized we had a little time left before he needed to be at the house.

"Dad, can we go to the mall and look at toys?"

"Sure, why not?"

So we stopped off at the mall and Todd began going down the aisles looking at everything. He stopped at the game section. There was a particularly interesting game he had his eye on. It was a baseball statistics game. He brought it over to me and said,

"Dad, can I get this one?"

I looked at the price: $30.

"Not today, son. You'll have to wait until your birthday or Christmas. I don't have any extra money right now."

I looked down at my watch and said, "Well, it's time to get you to your mother's."

He looked up at me and sighed.

"I guess we'll just have to make the best of it won't we, Dad?"

He had grown up a lot over the summer. At the tender age of seven, he had adjusted to what was needed to keep the peace.

We drove over to the house. My normal routine was to walk him up to the front door, give him a hug, and then go back to the car. I didn't hang around long because of the tension. It was tough enough without Reva and I getting into some ridiculous argument about nothing. As I walked him up to the door, Reva opened it before I could knock. This was highly unusual. Instead of saying anything nasty or slamming the door in my face or even giving me a scowl, she quickly invited me in. She was being very pleasant.

"Gary, why don't you come on in for a

minute? I would like to talk to you."

In the back of my mind, I thought she was setting me up for another surprise. Yet there was something different about her this time. There was a kindness.

"Sure, but I can't stay long."

"I know."

Then she turned to Todd and said, "Why don't you go upstairs and play in your room for a while. I need to talk to your dad for a few minutes, alone."

As soon as Todd was out of sight she turned to me and said, "Gary, I've been thinking about this divorce. I've been thinking about Todd and what is best for him, and I've decided that if you will agree with me on a couple of terms, he can stay with you."

She wanted to have joint custody and she wanted Todd and I to live with my parents. We were already living with them, and since my attorney said I didn't have a chance at anything except visitation, this "joint custody" idea was a bonus. I did my best to remain calm, but inside I was doing cartwheels.

"Sure, that would be great. Whatever you think is best."

As soon as I agreed she called up the stairs, "Todd, come down here for a minute. Momma has something to tell you."

He walked into the living room where she was standing and she pulled him aside. "Todd, I've decided the best thing for you is to live with your dad and grandparents. I will come and visit when I can, but I think this will be the best for all of us."

I was a little concerned about how he might react. I knew if he responded with too much glee, she might get angry and change her mind. I almost held my breath as he calmly looked up at her and said, "Okay, Mom, if that's what you want."

Perfect! He couldn't have done it better if I had coached him.

"Well, Todd, Momma's going to miss you, but I think this will be better in the long run. You go upstairs now and get your things that you'll need to move to your grandparents."

He immediately turned on his heels, ran up the stairs, grabbed his little suitcase, and ran back down. It couldn't have taken three minutes. She looked startled and said, "Is that it?"

"Yes, Mom, I've got what I need."

"What about your toys and your other clothes?"

"Grandma has plenty of toys and besides, I need to have some things here for when I visit you."

"Oh...okay, well, then I guess you'd better be going. Come on over here and give me a hug before you go."

He gave her a hug and said, "You know Mom, I was thinking. I know you are going to come and see me at Dad's. And I know this is not like I am going away for good, but just to live with Dad most of the time. I know you are going to see me again soon, but in a way this is kind of like I am leaving home, and I was wondering if you might want to give me a going away present?"

"What did you have in mind?"

"Well, Dad and I were at the mall today and there's a baseball game I wanted to get, but Dad said he couldn't afford it right now. But I was thinking maybe you would like to get it for me so I have something to remember you by."

I could tell by the look on her face she knew she was being set up, but under the circumstances, he did have the upper hand.

"Well, maybe. How much is it?"

"It's only $30 with tax."

"Thirty dollars! What kind of a game cost $30?"

"It's a special game, Mom. It would really mean a lot to me."

Hesitantly she said, "Well, okay."

She walked over to the coffee table to get her purse, pulled out $30, and handed it to Todd.

He practically ripped it from her hands, said a quick, "Thanks, Mom," and ran out the door screaming, "Come on Dad, we gotta go! The mall closes in fifteen minutes!"

I looked at her, shrugged my shoulders, and said, "Well, I guess we better go so he can get it before the store closes."

I almost couldn't drive because I was laughing so hard. What a little salesman Todd was. Three days later, all the paperwork was signed and now it became official. Todd was with me.

Chapter 11

A New Beginning

For some of you this might seem like a happy ending. Some would have said divorce was the best thing for all of us because of how horrible our home life had been. I've got an opinion about that. Divorce stinks. I don't care how we try to fluff it up or glaze it over; it's awful. In the Bible in the book of Malachi it says God hates divorce. My experience is that if God hates something, it is terrible for all concerned. I have never heard of a good divorce. My advice twenty years after mine, "Don't get divorced."

I don't care what it takes to make things right, don't get divorced. As much as I've tried to examine my situation and assure myself I did all I could to save my marriage, I'm still not convinced. Even after all these years, I still have to deal with moments of embarrassment and shame that would not be a part of my life had we made it work. Of course a good plan would be to pay attention to whom you are marrying in the first place. If a couple of your friends say you are marrying the Devil, perhaps you should hold off for a few more months before you take the leap. Another six months or even a year is not that long when it comes to making one of the most important decisions of your life. I believe that in my case, if we had waited another six months, I would have figured out that marriage was not a good decision.

Pay attention. Be sure God is putting your marriage together, and then keep your covenant with Him. I believe if we stand stronger and firmer in our commitments to God, we will see Him work more miracles in our lives. Often we hinder His deliverance because we take on our own deliverance. Instead of having an incredible testimony about God's healing and restoration, we settle for rationalized excuses of "I did the best I knew how."

I realize some of you reading this are already divorced. If that's you, do the best you can and don't make the same mistakes again. Yes, God can and will forgive divorce, but there are still consequences you have to live with.

In my case, some of the fallout included losing Shannon. She got bounced around from family to family during her high school years, and I ended up having little or no contact with her for quite a long time. Oh, I would try to visit and call her when I could, and of course I prayed for her, but it just wasn't good. She was always friendly and respectful, but it didn't feel like we were really connecting. It felt like she was drifting further and further away from me.

After the divorce was final the newest hurdle in my life was finding a good job. All I knew up to that point was sales. I did not have a college degree, and for whatever reason, I couldn't seem to find anything I could make a decent living at. Although I was relieved to be out of the vacuum-selling business, there were times I thought about some of the advantages it would bring financially. On one of those days the phone rang. It was my old boss. I thought I had made a complete escape from the world of sales, at least those vacuum cleaners. Yet, there I was, once again listening as he pushed the right buttons.

"Gary, it's good to hear your voice again."

"No, I'm not interested."

"What do you mean you're not interested? I haven't asked you anything yet."

"I know, but you didn't call to talk about the weather. I've known you too long for that. The only reason you would want to speak to me is if you thought I might be of some value to you, which means only one thing: You want me back in the business. I'm not interested."

"That's fine, Gary, let's not talk about the business, let's talk about you. How are you doing?"

"I'm doing fine."

"You are? That's great. So where are you working these days?"

"Right now I don't exactly have a job, but I'll find something."

"You're not working? Then how in the world could you be doing fine?"

"I'm doing fine except in that particular department of my life."

"Listen to me for a minute, Gary. I've got an idea I think you will like. Do you remember Don and Pauline?"

"You mean the farmers?"

"Good, so you do remember them. Here's the situation. They are trying to open an office and they need some help. They need somebody who knows the business and knows how to get a crew hired and on their feet. They've got plenty of money for inventory and they are great salespeople themselves. They just need a little direction. I was thinking you could work something out with them, nothing permanent, just for a few weeks. They'd be able to get a good start and you'd be able to make a few bucks until you find the job you're looking for."

He could have offered anything else in the world and I would have been able to turn it down, but I did remember those folks. We had met at several regional sales meetings over the years. I especially remembered how kind and honest they were. In fact, at that particular point in time they were the only people in the business I trusted. They had not been tainted by the slickness and temptations that seemed to grab the rest of us.

"Listen Gary, you don't have to make a decision right now. Think about it for a while and then let me know. Actually, let me give you their phone number and you can talk to them yourself. Just listen to them, it couldn't hurt."

"Okay, I'll think about it. But the truth is, I'm not interested."

Well, the truth was, I *was* interested because I wasn't working. If it hadn't been for Todd and I staying with my parents, I don't know how we would have survived. It was more than a little embarrassing not having a job and not carrying my weight. I had always worked and I hated how I felt not working.

I didn't think very long. In fact, I ended up calling Don and Pauline within the hour. We talked briefly on the phone, and they invited me to their house to "chat" about what might work. Within a couple of days I was back in the vacuum-selling business, and within a month I became a partner with them. For the first time I felt like I could make things work. Don and Pauline handled the money and I worked with the employees. I didn't have to worry about equipment, payroll, cash flow, or any of the details. All I had to do was focus on hiring, training, and developing salespeople, something which was as natural to me as falling down.

For the next several months we developed a pretty good team of salespeople and our new partnership was off to a good start. From a small business perspective, it looked like we might have ourselves a flourishing future together.

My finances improved; my self-worth improved: I enjoyed my work; Todd and I were doing well; and over all life became hopeful. The one thing still not going well was Shannon's circumstances. I never got over her leaving. I didn't talked about it much, but it ate away at me inside.

Since she was a ward of the state, I couldn't bring her back home with me. Although she did finally end up with a family that really loved and cared for her, I never felt good about my role in her life as a father. I tried to console myself by thinking, *It was her idea. She's the one who begged me to sign the paperwork.*

But that was a lame excuse. Why had I listened to a fourteen-year-old anyway? How could she possibly know what was best for her? It is difficult to analyze what exactly would have been the right thing to do. The only consolation was that those "bad" days had passed. In fact, over the course of the next few months, I was about to make the best decision of my life.

In the summer I decided to take a class on the Bible at a college in Kansas. A good friend of mine encouraged me to look for a friend of his while there. He didn't tell me much about her other than, "Her name is Susie."

I arrived at the campus on a Sunday. The class was to last two weeks. I planned to stay in a men's dorm while my parents took care of Todd, now nine years old, back in Indiana. I hadn't thought a lot about meeting this "Susie" until I arrived and realized out of six hundred people, I didn't know anyone. I looked around for her. It wasn't as if I was on a mission, so I took my time. I found her on Tuesday. I realize this sounds a little corny, but I actually felt like fireworks went off in my heart when we met. Of course, this made the situation more awkward than it needed to be. It is a very foolish thing to walk up to somebody and say, "Hi, I'm Gary, will you marry me?"

No, I didn't say that. I was able to manage some restraint and civility for the moment. Instead I took a less aggressive approach.

"Maybe we could talk a little later."

She responded by saying, "Sure, why don't we meet this afternoon by the pond during the afternoon break?"

"Yeah, sure, that would be great."

So I tracked her down that afternoon. Her account of that meeting was this "husky-looking" guy in the ugliest green shirt with red polyester shorts walked toward her. The funny thing to me was I thought I was dressed very "cool."

Hey, give me a break. I grew up in Indiana.

I tried not to act too interested, but inside my heart was exploding. I kept trying to tell myself I was overreacting and needed to get a grip. She seemed kind and was interested in talking about the things of God. Susan had been raised with a strong Catholic background, but had not come to know Jesus Christ in a personal way until about two years prior to our meeting.

This is an important concept to understand if you don't know it yet. A person can go to church, read the Bible, attend meetings, and even pray regularly, yet not know God in a real and personal way. There is a huge difference between knowing *about* someone and knowing them. There is also a huge distinction between knowing who Jesus Christ is and following Him.

Susan was like a little kid in a candy shop with her newfound faith in God. She talked about Jesus everywhere she went and often appeared like she was out to save the world all by herself. Some found this offensive. Some thought she was pushy and intrusive. Others looked to her as a lifesaver and heroine. I began to look at her as my future wife. Yet there was absolutely no way I could even hint as to the condition of my heart at such an early stage. We had only just met that day.

Over the course of the week we began to spend more and more time together. We talked for hours. Although we covered a large array of topics, they were all redirected toward things about God. This was very important to me, because I knew if there were to be any hope at all for a new relationship, my new wife would have to have a strong spiritual foundation. I wasn't about to settle for anything less.

The funny thing about this was I had actually had several talks with God over the previous year regarding remarriage. I had told Him many times that I was just fine remaining single for the rest of my life, yet knowing in my heart that He knew I didn't really want that. So about two weeks prior to meeting Susan, I threw out a very short prayer about this subject.

"Lord, you know how I have been telling you for months that I am happy to remain single for the rest of my life...and if that is truly Your plan for me, I want to be obedient. But I think we both know if somebody is out there who could love me like I need to be loved and somebody who loves you as much as I do, I would not be opposed to finding her. In fact, I'll just say it this way: If You do have somebody for me, I'm ready whenever You are."

And that was all I said. Up until that particular Tuesday, I had forgotten about my little talk. Surely He wasn't going to answer so quickly. Or was He?

I couldn't hide my emotions very long. We spent every spare moment together during the breaks between meetings. We ate breakfast, lunch, and dinner together. We went for long walks in the evenings, and I started thinking Susan was as interested in me as I was in her. But how could that be? There were a lot of differences in our backgrounds and even our current circumstances.

Finally I decided to tell her how I felt. There was a social event planned for Saturday night and I thought that would be the best time to say these things, because it would be somewhat like a date.

I got all dressed up that evening, which—I found out later—did not make much of an impression on Susan because I was fashionably challenged. Just as I was ready to walk out of my dorm, it hit me. I had forgotten to ask her to be my date for the evening. How could I be so foolish? My mind began to flash through several of the faces of the men who had also been talking to her throughout the week. What if one of them had asked her to be their date? She was very attractive. I kept saying to myself, *Gary, where is your brain? You cannot assume that because she has been spending so much time with you that she will automatically be with you this evening.*

I couldn't stand the thought of her being with somebody else. I literally ran to her dorm and waited in the stairwell for her to come down. (Men were not allowed in the women's dorms except in the entryways.) The stairwell wasn't air-conditioned. In fact, it was about ten degrees hotter than the temperature outside...and this was August in Kansas. I was sweating like a pig, waiting for Susan's arrival. I probably only stood there for about ten minutes, but it felt like hours. Finally, she came down and our eyes met. A girlfriend accompanied her, but as soon as the friend saw me, she got the message and excused herself.

We walked outside and I apologized profusely about my poor behavior in assuming she would attend the party with me. She didn't say much other than her surprise that I hadn't asked her, but she assumed we would see each other at the event. By the end of the evening I had forgotten my little speech. Instead of telling her I was attracted to her and hoped we could get to know each other better and keep in touch, I ended up saying, "Will you marry me?"

I felt like an idiot. *What am I thinking? I just met Susan four days ago. She must think I'm crazy. This will blow any possibility for this relationship. I wouldn't be surprised if she slapped me.*

And surprised I was.

She responded, "What took you so long?"

"What?"

"Yes, what took you so long? Why did you wait so long to ask me?"

And that was the beginning.

We married five months later in January. Susan was perfect for me. She was vibrant, exciting, fun, and full of life. She seemed to find the best in everyone. She could especially see the good in me. Some would call her an encourager; for me she became a life-giver. She was a cheerleader in high school and college, and she focused that same enthusiasm on me. Susan loved, encouraged, and supported me in almost every endeavor. She was very successful as a stockbroker. It was as if the word "failure" did not exist in her vocabulary, despite the reality that she had lived through some difficult times of her own.

Susan had been divorced for eleven years when I met her, and lived in Ohio with her two beautiful daughters. Melissa entered college that fall and Kelley was a junior in high school. Since Missy was an adult with Kelley not far behind, and they both had a great relationship with their father, the blended family situation for us was much easier to manage than most. Their adjustment to me was simple. I was the guy who married their mom. I didn't have to pretend to be some "new dad."

The biggest adjustment was between Todd and Susan, and overall that went well. He liked calling her Mom, and she never skipped a beat when it came to living out her role. Reva had visited Todd a couple of times, called a few times, and then lost contact. Reva's absence most likely made Susan and Todd's relationship that much smoother.

As wonderful as all of this was, life still had its challenges. For instance, we had to decide where to live. Since Susan had a lucrative job, the choice was simple: We chose her home in Ohio. Simple does not mean easy. It meant Todd had to move away from his grandparents, who were the only stabilizing force in his life to that point. He wasn't real crazy about the idea at first, but that's the way life works sometimes. The good news was that Susan poured herself into him right away, and we made arrangements for him to have some visits with my parents. All in all he adjusted quickly.

Another difficult issue was my work. I had to dissolve my partnership with Don and Pauline. They were disappointed at the time, but I think they were relieved after they realized how much money they were paying me. Besides, by then they knew as much or more about how to run the business as I did. So it proved a win - win.

Everything seemed to fall into place. Susan and I were happily married, Todd had a new mom, and I was able to start a new vacuum business in Ohio. The future looked bright. There was no reason for it not to be bright. Yet some things churning inside me had a way of derailing a seemingly perfect plan.

Chapter 12

Becoming a Big Shot

It is difficult to know exactly where the problem began, but without a doubt, it started long before I met Susan. Some of it had to do with pride, some with the embarrassment I attached to being a vacuum cleaner salesman, some with not finishing college, some with my failures as a father and husband, some with my lack of clear direction, and definitely some with the underlying knowing in my heart that I had not followed "the call."

The bottom-line issues? Self-esteem and self-worth. Every day felt like an uphill battle internally. It was as though a war was going on to defeat me at every turn, and I had to fight back with all that was within me, just to survive till the next day so I could start all over again. Nobody knew about this war, because I felt it was something I needed to handle myself. Let's face it, it dealt with my weaknesses and if a guy shares his weaknesses, how is talking about them going to help? I fell prey to the lie that talking would just be another sign of weakness. So I kept it a secret as best I could.

The interesting thing is many well-meaning,

innocent people in my life wounded me and were not even aware of it. I had become hypersensitive and consumed with my little world. When a person reaches such a point, he tends to think every conversation and every comment is directed at him in some manner. When I overheard Missy or Kelley say to Susan, "Mom, now what exactly does Gary do for a living?" my thoughts were, *Oh, they don't like me. They think I've got a rotten job. They think I'm taking advantage of their mom.* If someone talked about college, I thought, *I bet they think I'm a loser or stupid since I didn't get my degree.*

No matter what was said, if there was a way for me to read into it something negative about myself, I absorbed it. In the midst of all this, however, Susan—not knowing my thoughts—continued to build me up and talk about me as if she had married the greatest guy in the whole universe. You would think perhaps this would have balanced out my thinking to some degree, but it didn't seem to be enough.

On the other hand, when it came to spending time with my family and friends and business acquaintances, I was a completely different person. I was bold, confident, and often the life of the party. It was as if I lived two different lives in two different worlds.

Susan was a successful stockbroker. I was a struggling vacuum cleaner salesman. Susan owned a beautifully furnished house, nice clothes, and a Mercedes, and she belonged to a country club. I had no furniture or house, my clothes were polyester, I drove a dented up Volkswagen, and everything I owned fit in the backseat. Susan had lived in the same town her entire life, and knew everyone. I had moved fifteen times in the past seven years. Susan's idea of a good time was to attend the opera or ballet. Mine was to rent a good comedy. Susan savored fine dining. I was happy with a super-sized Number 3 and a Coke. Susan loved sushi. I preferred fish sticks. She liked tennis. I liked ping-pong. Probably the only thing we agreed on socially was our dislike of bowling.

The good news is I was a pretty cordial guy, so I sucked it up and went to the ballet once in a while. Susan was also happy to do some of the things I liked. I have to say it didn't take me long to buy into her ideas when it came to eating out. I quickly learned to enjoy fine dining. When it came to some of the other social gatherings, however, I still remained quite intimidated. I used to think, *If I could just get into a different line of work, something respectable, then life would be better. People would respect me more.*

I hated that Susan made more money than I did...not out of jealousy, but out of a sense of inadequacy. Down deep I wanted to take care of her. Soon after we were married I realized she hated her job and would have preferred to stay at home and be a wife and mother. She was tired from being the sole provider all those years on her own and I think she hoped I would take the lead in these matters. Knowing this caused me to work harder, put in longer hours, and look for ways that Susan could get out of her situation. But no matter how much I tried, it didn't work.

I was a distributor, which meant other salespeople worked under me and I made commissions from their sales. The business was like a roller coaster. I sometimes cleared as much as $14,000 per month, only to follow up with three or four months of losses. The only consistency was inconsistency. The high turnover of the sales staff and my hatred of the business both contributed to this. Sure, I loved it when it was going well, but since I had more months of losses than gains, I pretty much hated it all the time. A good question here would be, "Then why did you stay in that business?"

The truth was threefold. One, I was afraid to get out because I didn't have any confidence that I could do anything else. Two, every time I thought about getting out, I'd have several sales in a row and would think, *Let's get real, Gary. Where is a guy with your background and education going to find a job making $3,000 a week?*

And three, the breaking of number five, "Honor your father and your mother." Yes, I got along with them. Yes, I was kind to them. Yes, our relationship had become much better, but there was still a wedge between us. In my heart I was still in rebellion against them. They didn't know it and I never talked about it, but I still thought I knew better than they did. Also, I never asked their forgiveness for my past decisions and always expected them to adjust to my thinking.

Whatever I touched seemed to be cursed in some way. Just as I began to lose hope, a new opportunity opened up.

The vacuums sold for around $1,000. Many of our customers could not afford to pay cash, so we sold the contracts to a local finance company. This was a common practice with "in home" sales businesses. We would sell the product, fill out a credit application, fill out a contract for terms of payment, then turn it over to a finance company, and they would collect the payments. We received our money from the finance company within three to five days after the credit check was approved.

On one occasion of selling the contracts, something terrible happened. We sold five vacuums, filled out all the paperwork, turned it in, got the contracts approved, and delivered the product to the customers. The day I was to be paid for these sales, I walked into the finance company and the manager said, "Oh, hi Gary. I bet you came in today to get your money? Well, we've got a little problem. It seems the home office has decided to cancel all 'in home' sales agreements. For the time being, we will no longer be able to handle your contracts."

"I don't understand."

"It is a change in policy. It's a state-wide decision."

"What am I supposed to do?"

"You'll have to find alternative financing."

"Well, that stinks."

"Yeah, I know, but I'm sure it's just a temporary situation. If there is anything I can do to help get you set up with another company, I'd be happy to help."

"Thanks, but I'm pretty sure there are a couple of other companies I can work with. So, I guess this is my last check from you for a while?"

"No, Gary, you misunderstand. I don't have a check for you today. In fact, I'm going to have to return those contracts and you'll have to see if you can get someone else to buy them."

"You can't even pay me on what's already been approved?"

"Sorry, no."

"This is awful. I've already delivered the machines. I've got salespeople expecting me to bring them a paycheck today."

"I know it puts you in a tough situation, but it's out of my hands."

"All right, give me the contracts."

I left that finance company and went down the street to another one. Though they were happy to take me on as a dealer, they said it would take thirty to forty-five days to get me set up. This was very bad news. I needed the money that day.

I sat in my office bemoaning my situation when I got a thought, *Randy. It's a long shot, but just maybe he could help me out this once.*

I picked up the phone and called him. Susan and Randy had recently become partners as stockbrokers. Randy had the money, but I didn't know if he would be interested. We had also become good friends over the past couple of years and I knew if a good business deal were in the mix, it would make my proposition even better.

"Hello, Randy?"

"Oh, hi Gary, how are you doing?"

"Well, I'm not doing so great today. I've got myself into a tough situation and I was wondering if you might be able to help me out. It would be a good deal for you if you were interested."

"Well, tell me what you have in mind."

I went through the whole scenario, then explained why it was a sound business opportunity for him.

"Here's how it could be good for you. If you buy the contracts, I will collect the payments and pay you a great return for the use of the money. The finance company charges twenty four percent. I would be happy to guarantee you sixteen percent and I would keep the other eight percent for my trouble in doing the collections."

Before I could say anything more, he said, "How about I just loan you the money personally and you work out the details on your end?"

"Sure, that would work."

"Well, come on down to my office and I'll give you a check."

My problem was solved. We made an agreement that he would loan me the money and I would loan the money to my company. That way he didn't have to worry about any problems with the contracts or any concerns with his business.

It was simply a personal loan to me. The contracts were my problem.

It looked like I would be fine. I would have my new financing set up in a few weeks, and in the mean time we would just encourage other customers to get their own financing. I also knew a couple of vacuum distributors who said they could help me for the interim, so it appeared that I'd get over this hurdle much easier than I expected. A couple of days later, the phone rang. It was Randy again.

"Listen Gary, I've been thinking about our arrangement. If you are interested, I have some more money I'd be willing to loan you if you can offer me the same return."

"Are you serious?"

"Of course I'm serious."

"Well, sure, I'd love to keep this going."

So that was the beginning of one of the potentially greatest opportunities of my life. It all seemed so simple. It was a great deal for both of us. Before, I had to wait three to five days to receive money from the contracts. Now every sale was like a cash sale because Randy didn't require me to wait.

Well, there were at least two major problems with this same-day service. First, this "cash flow" belief system was a lie. Waiting three to five days had nothing to do with being successful. Second, I was now in charge of approving all the loans instead of a third party. This created several new issues, one being that I found it difficult to turn anyone down. I was too soft.

A salesman would bring me a credit application. I would get it checked out. When approval was borderline, I would attempt to turn it down. But the salesmen were not only good at selling vacuums, they were good at selling me on why they "knew" the customer would pay. Often they accompanied their pitch with a sympathy speech about how they desperately needed their commission check. The business was notorious for attracting salespeople who lived on the edge of financial ruin. So, with my motives of wanting to boost sales and my weakness for a sad story, I became more and more lenient with my approvals.

Another new problem that developed was my sympathy toward some of my friends. Several of them approached me for a loan to help them out of financial pinches. At first I told them my company was not a bank or even a regular finance company. All of our loans had to be accompanied by the sale of a vacuum cleaner. Then one friend suggested I write up a contract for him to purchase a vacuum, but skip the delivery.

"Listen, Gary, nobody will even know I don't have one of the vacuum cleaners. Just loan me $1,000, I'll make the payments, and no one will be the wiser."

I knew it was a bad idea, but some of my friends were very persuasive, and I felt pretty good about myself, helping them out. It didn't take long before the word got out that Gary could fix your financial woes as long as it was under $1,000. Of course, in my state of mind, I didn't want to bother Randy with the details of my decisions, nor did I want to own up to the fact that I was setting myself up to fail again. So I created a secret world.

If Randy asked, "How's everything going with the loans?" I'd say, "Everything is going great."

That was what I hoped for, at least. Only one thing *had* to happen for this to work long term: Everybody needed to fulfill his or her contract. Within a couple of months, several of the loans became difficult to collect. And my friends? They were the worst when it came to paying on time. Oh sure, Gary was real popular when they needed some help with rent, but when it came time to pay Gary back, there were always excuses. Plus, I was too easy on them. If they whined a little, I just said, "Well, do the best you can and pay me as soon as possible."

I was foolish.

A few months later I got a call from Randy. "Gary, I've got some bad news. I'm not going to be able to loan you anymore money for a while."

"That's okay, don't worry about it," I said. "I've got my other financing set up and so we'll just go back to doing business like we did before. It's not a problem. Thanks for all your help for all this time."

I cannot begin to explain in words how happy this made me. This was the best news that could have come my way. I wouldn't have any choice anymore in making loans. All I had to do was collect the deals that were out there, and over the next couple of years my mess would be fixed. All Randy would ever know is that he loaned me some money and I paid him back and working with Gary was a good thing. I had dodged a bullet.

A few days passed and I got another call from Randy. "Gary, I've got an idea. Let's start our own finance company. We'll put together a business plan, take it to the bank, and have them loan us the money at a couple of points over prime. Then we'll loan the money out at the same rate as the other finance companies and we'll split the profits. You can be the manager of the finance company, find someone else to run your company, and then you'll be out of the vacuum business that you hate so much. It will be a great deal for both of us."

I was in a tough spot. I couldn't deny that I would love to be doing something else careerwise, and this sounded a lot more prestigious than my current occupation. Plus, Randy seemed to be successful at everything he got involved with. When it came to money, he just had a knack for making more. Not to mention the fact that if I turned him down he'd ask why. What was I going to tell him, that I had made a bunch of lousy loans with his money and it was going to consume all of my spare time to make things right? That would have been a bad day. So I said what any red-blooded, prideful, "want-to-be-successful" guy would say, "That sounds great. I'd love to."

Chapter 13

Unraveling

Predator: One that victimizes, plunders, or destroys, especially for one's own gain.

I suppose now is as good a time as any to talk about predators. I have casually mentioned this word before in reference to Raymond the homosexual, Carl the pimp, and my ex-wife. Now a new predator is entering the story, and his name is Gary. Yes, I'm talking about myself. No, I didn't start out as a predator, but of course none of the others did either. And, as I've said, it is very important to pay attention to who you hang around with, because one of two things will happen: Either your friends will rise up to your standards or you will sink down to theirs. It works every time. A good rule of thumb is to spend time with folks who are living at a higher moral standard than you are.

It is interesting to see how a person can change for the worse so easily. It doesn't usually happen overnight. Often others see such changes, but for some reason the person on the downward slide is the last to find out. One learns how to justify his own actions, words and even thoughts—

which is what I learned well, to fake myself out. Not only do the changes come gradually, the consequences don't immediately erupt either. This creates another problem: If one doesn't get strong correction right away, he tends to go in deeper than he should, sometimes to the place where he can't get out.

It is important for you to know that throughout my life I held two very strong convictions. I loathed both liars and thieves. I never cheated on a test or even thought about stealing a piece of candy. To me, honesty was the most important attribute a person could have. This is why none of my handling of business made any sense, except in my mind's rationalization.

Randy and I formed our finance company. He signed personally for the loan at the bank, and it was now up to me to make it work. I was determined to do it right. I spent several days thinking about it and decided to keep everything clean from this point forward. Besides, safety nets were in place. The bank monitored the payments. A professional accounting firm audited our company every three months, and an accountant approved all checks before they were given to me. It sounded like a perfect plan.

Yet somehow I was able to manipulate things to keep the accountant happy, sidestep the auditors, and keep the loan officer at bay. I'm not proud of it, and wasn't then. The truth be known, I had no grand scheme in mind. All of the decisions I made in maneuvering around the system were birthed out of desperation and survival, not with the intention of scamming anyone. I would cross any boundary to cover my poor decisions. I was consumed with keeping appearances favorable.

Even though I tried to do things right with this fresh start, in many ways I was already in trouble. All of the previous loans I had made were transferred under the new finance company, which included ones I had made to friends and other loans I never should have made. I tried to look into ways to keep these old loans separate, but ultimately, the bank insisted they be wrapped into the new agreement. Of course neither the bank nor Randy knew the loans were problematic. To bring that up would have ruined their support, not to mention the devastation to our friendship.

One thing I thought would help bail me out was to hire someone to manage the vacuum cleaner company. This would allow me to focus on collections. However, it proved to be a huge mistake. The man I hired—or a salesman under him—sold thousands of dollars worth of equipment out the back door over the next several months. Had I been paying closer attention, I would have noticed a discrepancy right away, but I was too busy manipulating the paperwork for my own problems.

On the collections side, I juggled the paper trail by falsifying contracts and making some of the payments for the customers who were delinquent. The purpose of this was to buy myself some time until I got enough profits from the sales company to clear it all up. And it worked, at least temporarily. I justified my actions by rationalizing, *All Randy cares about is getting his percentage. All the bank cares about is getting their percentage. All the auditing company cares about is the numbers working out.*

All I cared about was being respected and loved, and it was happening. Everyone treated me like a king. I became a hotshot entrepreneur almost overnight.

Then the cards began to fall. Not right away, but little by little. Obviously, the equipment that went out the back door incurred losses, plus some of the original loans completely defaulted. To compound the problem, the loans I had made to friends ended up becoming gifts from me because my friends just couldn't seem to stick to our agreement.

My dilemma was obvious. I couldn't tell anyone about the loans defaulting or the auditors would dissect everything. I couldn't tell anyone about the loans to my friends because I wasn't authorized to make those loans. I couldn't expose the thief in my own ranks because that too would have sounded an alarm which I wasn't prepared to handle.

My only hope was to shut the whole thing down and then work like a dog to pay it all back. I called a special meeting with Randy and planned to confess everything. But when we met, I wasn't man enough to tell him the truth. I did complain that this was a lot more work than I had anticipated and I didn't know if I could keep the finance company going. He said it didn't make any sense to stop now because it was just a matter of time before we would both be rich. I thought, *Rich? What a joke. If he only knew, he'd kill me.*

"Gary, the bank is really pleased with how you handle everything. They are even talking about buying us out someday. It could be in the millions. What can I do to help? Do we need to hire somebody to assist you? It is working so well, it would be crazy to let this go."

I tried to open my mouth and say the words that needed to be said, but I found myself saying, "No, we don't need to hire anyone yet. I'll make some adjustments with the sales company, and I'm sure within a couple of months I'll be able to manage it much better."

At that point I was working between eighteen and twenty hours a day, seven days a week. Between the bank, the auditors, the accountant, and the sales company, it took a lot of time to make all the pieces fit. I thought I was losing my mind. When Randy and I talked, I was trying to cover for between $90,000 and $100,000.

At the height of my insanity I found myself saying things like, "All I need is a little break here and I'll be right back on top." I sounded like someone with a gambling addiction. You know, it starts small. You win a little; you lose a little, no big deal. Then you lose more than you planned. The next thing you know you're cashing in your retirement savings and selling your house. It's a crazy world when it gets to that point. My problem was I couldn't cash in or sell anything because I needed to keep up the act.

There was absolutely no way I could tell Susan. All she knew was I worked long hours and suffered from a little stress. I dug in, determined to make things work. But it just got worse. I started approving every sale, thinking I could worry about collections later. I tried everything I knew to build up the business and put the money back, but it kept spiraling downward, out of control. Over the next several months the losses grew to more than $300,000.

I thought to myself, *I've got to stop. I can't fix this. Something has to change. I've got to force myself to stop.*

But I couldn't.

Some of you might say, "Why couldn't you stop?"

Well, that's like saying to an alcoholic, "Just stop drinking."

Or to a chain smoker, "Just stop smoking."

Most people with these addictions will tell you it is like trying to stop a freight train going a hundred miles an hour. It's not that easy.

Finally, I came up with a plan. It wasn't a great plan, but at least it was a plan. I thought if I could get out of the finance business, I could cut off my source to this addiction. If I didn't have access to money, I couldn't do anything wrong with it. As horrible as things were, I thought I could pay everything off in five to seven years if I focused on the vacuum cleaner sales. I needed $9,000 each month to cover payments on all the loans. I knew that would be incredibly difficult, if not impossible, but if I could at least come up with $3,000 to $4,000 a month, it would be enough to keep the bank happy. They would just tack on the balance at the end of the loan and earn more interest. I could tell them I was having some collection problems and I needed some extra time to pay off the loans. As long as I was consistent and the bank collected their interest, I knew they would be satisfied. I just couldn't have any bad months of sales.

As I mentioned earlier, I had experienced some successful months of $12,000 to $14,000, so if I even raked in half that, there would be enough to live off of and pay back these loans. The problem was how to shut the whole thing down without making everybody nervous.

I got the idea from the bank, somewhat by accident. When I tried to make a loan to someone out-of-state, the bank called and said it was illegal for our finance company to loan anywhere other than in Ohio. This was my out. I thought, *I'll just move to another state. Then we'll have to shut down the finance company because I am the only one who can run it. All I have to do is figure out where and why to move. Plus I need to convince Susan and Randy that moving is a great idea.*

Where didn't really matter to me at the time, but when Susan and I took a vacation in Colorado,

I knew it was the answer. While we were there I started talking to her about moving.

"Isn't it great out here? It is so beautiful. Listen, Kelley's off to college next fall. It's just you, Todd, and I. Why don't we move out here? We could sell the house back home, buy a house here, I could forget about that finance company and just go back to selling. I could open up a vacuum cleaner distributorship here and we could probably work it out for you to get out of the brokerage business. You know you hate it. Wouldn't it be great?"

Well, she didn't go for it right away, but within a couple of days we started looking at some homes and talking more about the possibilities. I hate to admit this, but if I remember correctly, I think I even told her something like, "I believe this move is what God would want us to do."

I realize saying such a thing is about as low as I could get. But on the other hand, if I was so fouled up in my mind as to justify losing over $300,000, I probably wouldn't have much of a problem rationalizing that it was God's will for us to move. Especially since I believed it was the only way to force myself to stop making things worse. I don't remember the details of our conversations after that, but I do remember we put an offer on a house, went home, sold our house in about ten days, and were on the road to Colorado a couple of months later.

Convincing Randy was easier than I thought. Once I had Susan on board and brought to the table that I was on a mission from God, he didn't put up much of a fight. All I had to do now was get my sales company up and running, pour everything I knew into it, and get this all behind us. Best of all, nobody would lose and nobody would have to know.

I was both relieved and excited. I felt like I was on the road to recovery. I knew it was going to be tough, but at least I was headed in the right direction. What I wasn't prepared for was the quick downturn emotionally once I set up my new business in Colorado. I became paralyzed with fear. This caused a chain reaction throughout my company. I am a firm believer in the philosophy that work breeds work and sales breeds sales. These attitudes become contagious. I, however, fell prey to another philosophy: fear breeds fear and failure breeds failure.

I knew how to sell; yet I couldn't. I set up appointments and drove to the people's houses, only to become so paralyzed with the fear of not being able to sell that I could hardly make myself open the car door. This attitude rubbed off on my sales team, and they couldn't sell. It was as though every second ticked aloud in my mind, waiting for the bomb to explode. I became afraid of everything. I was afraid to answer the phone in fear that it might be the bank or Randy. I was afraid to open my mail in fear of some lawsuit. I was afraid to wake up. I hid under the covers early in the morning thinking if I got out of bed, they'd all be waiting just outside my door to haul me away.

I had earned thousands a month in my glory days and now I couldn't scrape together enough change for lunch. We fell behind in our car and house payments. I had trouble keeping up with my office lease. Anything involving money deteriorated.

What surprised me the most was it took over nine months for the truth to surface. Somehow I kept the bank and everyone else satisfied with my excuses and half-truths. It felt like I was singing, tap dancing, and juggling all at the same time. A guy can only keep that kind of thing going for a time before he can't fake it anymore. The moment of truth will always come, and it came for me as well. When it did, it was a very, very, bad day.

Chapter 14

The Truth Hurts

I remember hiding out in my basement late in the evenings for literally hours, praying, begging for a miracle. Surely there had to be some way out. There had to be some method, some plan, something I hadn't thought of yet. I still hoped I'd get a break.

I was sitting in the living room on a Saturday evening and the phone rang. It was a friend of mine I hadn't seen for almost a year, who used to work for me. Apparently, Randy had questioned him about some concerns he had regarding our business.

My friend's remarks were brief and to the point. "Gary, I just met with Randy. I need to tell you, I've never seen anyone so angry in my entire life. I think he might be headed to Colorado to see you real soon. You're in for a rough time. I think he'd like to kill you."

I just sighed and thanked him for the call. No, I wasn't concerned that Randy would kill me. I knew this was just my friend's interpretation. I did, however, feel like I was walking to the end of a gangplank. It was all very surreal. At that point nothing really surprised me, because I'd been waiting for this day for over a year and a half. Every morning, the first thing that came to my mind was, "I wonder if I'll make it through today without being exposed?"

Even so, I felt unprepared for what might happen. I needed some words of wisdom. I immediately thought of Terry. Terry was a good friend and my pastor. Susan and I had attended his Bible studies for a year. He was kind, patient, and always seemed to have a level head about himself. I raced to his house.

Getting advice this late in the game wasn't the best. It was like trying to reach for a seatbelt while flying out of a windshield. It definitely wasn't fair to Terry to put him in a place of decision. I was hoping he might have some revelation from God. God wasn't talking to me these days, or at least I wasn't hearing Him.

I pulled into the driveway and rang the doorbell. Terry's wife answered and led me to a side room where Terry and I could talk privately. I told him the whole mess as best I could in about ten minutes. He remained calm, but direct.

"Does Susan know about this?"

"No."

"Get in your car right now and get home. Sit her down and tell her everything. I don't know what to tell you yet about the business, but your only hope for saving your marriage is if Susan hears it from you first. If she hears it from Randy or anyone else, you can forget about keeping her. After the two of you have talked, you are welcome to come back here and we'll discuss it together in more detail."

I thanked him and drove home. I knew he was right. I walked in the door, asked Susan to sit down, and told her the whole story. I hated that I'd let Randy down. I hated that I'd been so foolish. I hated everything connected to this life I'd been leading. Yet all of that paled in comparison to how I hated letting Susan down. She trusted me. I failed her.

Her response was unbelievable. She remained calm, though a little confused because in my rambling confession I didn't make a lot of sense. She asked a lot of questions, trying to put the pieces together. Overall, she was amazing. She didn't talk down to me or say anything to make me feel worse than I already did. Of course that would not have been possible anyway. A guy can only go so low.

I knew Susan had been aware for several months that things were not going very well, but I always reassured her, "Don't worry, it's all going to turn around. Everything is going to be all right."

In no way was she prepared for this catastrophe. It was far worse than she could have imagined.

We agreed to take the initiative right away. We couldn't wait for Randy to call or show up on our doorstep. Susan said, "Gary, Randy and I were partners. I know him better than you do. Let me speak to him first."

"No, I need to make that call."

"Listen, Gary, if he's as angry as you think he might be, he's angry at you, not me. So let me talk to him first and then you can say what you need to say."

I didn't really trust myself to make any decision at that moment. I was a basket case. Susan made the call in another room. After what seemed like a half hour or so, I got on the phone. He was calm but firm.

"Gary, I want you and Susan to fly to Ohio on Monday. We're going to sit down and look at the whole picture. It's time for you to come clean on this. I want you to tell me everything, no holding back."

"Yes, sir, I will. Randy, I'm so, so, sorry."

Never before did I have the sense that the word "sorry" meant so little.

"I'll see you and Susan on Monday."

Click.

I asked Susan if she would go with me to talk to Terry. She immediately agreed. In some ways I felt a lot lighter now that there weren't any more secrets. In fact, I had a fresh hope that Terry would have an answer or a strategy to make everything just fine.

The first thing he did was to look at Susan. In a stern, direct manner, Terry said, "Susan, before we get into the details of this ordeal I need to know something. Are you going to stick with Gary through this or not? I won't blame you if you don't because this might get very messy, but you do need to make a decision right now. Either you are with Gary or you're not. If you are, you can stay and listen. If you're not, I'll have to ask you to wait in the other room while I talk to Gary alone."

She was silent for a few seconds before responding, "Yes, I'm going to stick with Gary, no matter what."

Terry had just saved my marriage. Not because of what was happening in the present, but because of what we would face in the future.

Then Terry turned to me and said, "Okay, Gary, let's start from the beginning."

I proceeded to give he and Susan the details, and it felt good to get all of this out into the open. The next words out of Terry's mouth, however, were not comforting.

"Gary, you've gotten yourself in a really big mess. I'd like to help you, but I don't know how. The only way I could possibly help is if you and Randy were willing to sit down with myself or some other non-biased person, and agree to handle the situation according to the counsel given. Otherwise, my counsel to you at this time is no counsel. The only thing I can suggest is that you get the best lawyer you can and Randy get the best lawyer he can and let them fight it out. You're in a real mess."

As much as it hurt, I appreciated that he told me the way it was rather than build up false hope in me.

We thanked him for his time and headed home. The next couple of days were very difficult. Susan had a lot of questions, but I didn't want to talk, not because I was trying to be inconsiderate; I just didn't want to talk. I still hoped I would wake up and none of this would be true.

Monday came quickly. Susan and I boarded a plane. During the flight, I decided to write out my confession, hoping Randy would have some compassion for me. I was an emotional wreck. We arrived in the afternoon and rented a car to drive to his house. Just as we were getting ready to get out of the car, Randy walked up and began talking to Susan. He didn't look at me or talk to me, he just said, "I'm not interested in hearing any more of Gary's lies. I have set up an appointment for him at the bank tomorrow and I want him to tell them everything."

I begged him to at least read my confession, but he said, "Tell it to them. I'm not interested."

Then he turned and walked away. Obviously something had changed between Saturday and Monday. It was clear that any proposition to meet with a non-biased party to negotiate would not be received very well.

We backed out of his driveway and started discussing what Randy had demanded. It didn't sound like a good idea, talking to the bank. I became more and more concerned, so we talked to some friends who encouraged us to find an attorney and get legal advice.

I found someone who was supposed to be pretty good at this kind of thing and gave him the overview of the situation. He said, "No, Gary, do not go spill your guts to the bank. They could have video cameras or some other recording devices there and it could put you in a very tough spot. Tell me who you are supposed to meet with and I'll get it cancelled. Let's meet tomorrow in my office. You can give me the whole story then, and we'll see what we need to do to get this cleaned up."

Part of me sighed a sigh of relief. I was going to have a professional represent me. I knew I wasn't in any state of mind to do a very good job of representing myself. Another part of me, however, just wanted to get it all out and move on with my life, no more secrets and no more strategies. This felt like a strategy. I thought, *Why can't I just come clean and start paying everybody back? I'll make it right if they'll just give me a chance.*

We met with the attorney the next morning. After he heard the story he said, "Don't worry about this Gary, this is just a partnership problem. We just need to do some negotiating."

"Will it go to court?"

"I doubt it. We should be able to work it out between the two of you. But even if it does, there's nothing to worry about. It's a civil matter. You might have to pay some fines and work out some kind of restitution, but this is nothing serious. It's just a civil dispute between two partners, nothing criminal."

What a relief.

We never did meet with the bank, and my attorney sent us home, saying he'd call us in a few days after he met with Randy and his attorney. A week or so passed before I heard from him. "I've got some bad news for you, Gary. They've decided to turn this whole thing over to the prosecution and they are going to try and come after you criminally. Now don't worry, I don't think they have a leg to stand on. You just hold tight and I'll let you know as it begins to unfold."

"I thought it was going to be a civil suit at the worst!"

"Yeah, I know, that's what I thought too. Don't worry, they don't have a thing on you that will hold up."

"Are you sure?"

"Yeah, pretty sure."

I wasn't convinced.

After that phone call, my stomach knotted up, and that knot didn't go away for several months. I continued to pray and beg God for some kind of miracle, but there didn't seem to be one on the horizon.

Over the next couple of weeks I received phone calls from some friends who used to work for me. They were being interrogated by the prosecutor's office. Some were even told they would be brought up on charges with me.

"Gary, I don't know what to tell them. They say I was in on this with you. They say there is no way you could have done this by yourself and that I had to know and must have helped you. Gary, I don't know what to do. I don't even understand their questions. What did you do, anyway?

I don't want to get you into any trouble. We're friends."

"Just tell them the truth and don't worry about me. They are only fishing."

After we hung up I felt horrible. It had never occurred to me that they would attack my friends. At first I thought, *Let them do their little interrogation; my friends don't have anything to hide. If they tell the truth, they'll be okay.*

Then it hit me.

Gary, what kind of friend are you anyway? How can you let others be put through this when in reality you *should be taking the heat for this? It is not right for your friends to have to suffer because of your foolishness. You need to stand up and be a man. You need to take responsibility for your actions, confess the truth, and let the pieces fall where they may. You can't hide behind a system and hope your silence will make this all work out. You value your friends too much to make them go through any more than they already have.*

I called Terry.

"I was thinking of confessing. My actions are not right. I need to stand up and be a man and take whatever comes. I have been praying more than ever before and I don't feel like I am handling this like God would want me to. I feel like the right thing for me to do is to come clean, all the way."

Terry said something I'll never forget.

"Gary, the world may never understand what or why you are making this decision, but God knows. He will always know, and He's the only one who really matters. You may go your entire lifetime and not see any fruit of this decision, but God will reward you in eternity for doing the right thing. That may be your only consolation."

I knew as soon as I'd talked to Terry that this was right, so I called my attorney and gave him the news. At first he tried to talk me out of it, but even I could tell it was a half-hearted effort. I sensed that down deep this was good news for him because everything he had promised had blown up in his face. He did, however, make one more promise. He promised to get me a good deal.

"Gary, I'll contact the prosecutor tomorrow. The worst that will happen is you'll probably get five years probation. You will have a permanent blemish on your record, but aside from that you'll be just fine. I'll let you know what the next step is in a couple of days."

He called me back after he'd made arrangements for me to give my deposition to the prosecution and go before the judge. So, Susan and I packed up the car and drove back across country to meet with them.

It went as well as I could have expected. I sat across the table from three or four prosecutors while they asked me a lot of questions. I was straight up with them on everything. My next meeting was with the judge. I pled guilty to the crime. She set sentencing for sixty days later and I was sent downstairs to fill out some paperwork.

It all went quickly. I was asked a couple of

questions, handed a paper to sign, and let go. They didn't even require me to post bond. All I had to do was sign a paper, promising to return for the sentencing. My attorney was very happy.

"Gary, that is a very good sign. They didn't even ask for any kind of bond. They always ask for a bond, especially when you live out of state. You are going to be just fine."

Susan and I headed back to Colorado to wait out the sixty days. We were running a little short on finances, so we had to drive to these meetings instead of fly, which was about a two-day trip each way. Susan was amazing. She kept encouraging me and telling me how much she loved me and that everything was going to work out, that no matter what, we'd get through all of this.

"Gary, never forget: We've got God and each other and that is all that matters."

It sounded kind of cheesy in a way, but I didn't care. I needed some cheese.

The next two months seemed to drag out forever. The suspense of not knowing the exact outcome was more than a little disturbing. Finally it was time to go back. The first thing I did was meet with my attorney and prepare myself for the worst.

"Okay, now let's go over this one more time. After tomorrow I'll be on probation for five years, right?"

"Yeah, that's what I think they are going to give you."

"You think. You mean you don't know for

sure?"

"Listen, Gary, we never know for sure until the judge makes the call in the courtroom, but yes, I'm fairly confident you're going to get five years probation."

"What if it's something else? What if they decide to go ballistic on me? What's the worst that can happen?"

"The worst? I suppose the worst would be they'd give you Pete Rose."

"Pete Rose, what's Pete Rose?"

"What I mean is, they'd give you what they gave Pete Rose, ninety days on a farm camp somewhere."

"What?! You told me I'd get probation, five years probation. What's this Pete Rose stuff?"

"Calm down, Gary. You asked me what the worst-case scenario could be and that's it. Just relax. I'm sure it's going to be the probation."

"Listen, I can't do Pete Rose. I've never been in jail before. I can't do it. I've never had anything but a couple of speeding tickets. I can't do jail. I can't do ninety days. I can't do Pete Rose!"

"Gary, just cool it. You're going to be fine."

I wasn't comforted at all by this news. That night I went for a long walk trying to hear from God, hoping He would comfort me or give me a hint that what I feared the most would not happen. He was silent. I didn't blame Him.

The next morning, Susan and I met with the attorney one last time before we went into the courtroom. I asked him again if he knew any more. He had nothing to add. We walked into the courtroom and sat down. A couple of our friends were there with us. We all sat in silence waiting for my turn before the judge. My attorney said he needed to go to the judge's chambers for a few minutes and that he'd be right back. Fifteen minutes later he returned, his face was as white as a sheet. He sat down next to me, but he wouldn't look at me and he didn't want to talk.

"What happened in there?"

"Well, Gary, it didn't go so well."

"Oh, no. I'm going to get Pete Rose. No, this can't be happening. I'm going to get Pete Rose aren't I?"

"Let's just wait and see what happens."

"I'm getting Pete Rose, I just know it."

"Gary, let's wait and see."

"How can I possibly do ninety days in jail? I'm not ready for this."

The judge finally called me. I walked up to a podium to state my name and answer several routine questions, and then wait for the sentence. I was still praying and hoping that somehow I'd get a break.

Then it happened, the moment of truth. I don't recall much of what the judge said or asked. The whole day seemed like a fog. What I do remember with clarity were her final words.

"By the power invested in me, by the state of Ohio, I hereby sentence you, Gary Skinner, to four to fifteen years in a state penitentiary. Bailiff, take him away."

My mind became numb. I thought, *What did she just say? Did I hear her right? Did she say four to fifteen years? I can't believe my ears. This has got to be some kind of rotten dream. Lord, please tell me it's not true. Please wake me up. No. This cannot be real.*

The bailiff walked me out of the courtroom and handcuffed me. We started walking down a hallway that seemed more like a tunnel, because my head was caving in. As I waited for him to open a door, I looked to my left and down another hallway and saw Susan. I'll never forget the look on her face. You see, since we first met she had this dream for us, that we were going to be this team for God, her and I. At that moment all I could see was disappointment, pain, confusion, and hopelessness in her eyes. Shame and despair immediately engulfed me.

How could it have gone so far? How could I have been so foolish?

Chapter 15

A New Guy on the Block

A lot of things raced through my mind as I looked at Susan in the hallway. It seemed like I had died. Of course I have no idea what that is like since I've never died, but that is what I was thinking. I was leaving everything I knew in this world and in this life to go to another one somewhere. In my case it didn't have the prospects of heaven.

The next few hours were terrible. They escorted me downstairs to a room where I had to turn in my street clothes—which in my case was a fairly nice pinstriped suit—for what would be my new wardrobe. They handed me a blue pullover with a v-neck, a pair of blue pants that looked somewhat like hospital pants that doctors wear, and some silly looking shower shoes. They removed the handcuffs, fingerprinted me, and had me sit on a bench next to another guy waiting to be processed.

We were both there for about a half-hour, but it seemed like a lot longer to me because the guy wouldn't shut up. For some reason he thought I was his audience and he was determined to wear me out with his nonsensical blabbering.

"What ya in here for?"

"I'd rather not talk about it."

"They got me on a B&E and some kinda assault thing. I don't think they are going to be able to keep me here very long, 'cause I didn't do much 'cept stab the guy in the gut. In fact, he's already outta the hospital."

I just looked at him. I didn't have a clue what to say, nor was I in the mood to make any new friends. I thought, *What am I doing here? Why am I with the likes of this guy? What does he mean, "all he did was stab a guy in the gut"? He's acting as though that was nothing.*

The truth be known, he got a lighter sentence than I did.

Finally, they called my name and escorted me down another hallway to an examination room. A doctor asked me some medical questions for their records. After about a half-hour of that, they took me to another room filled with old grungy-looking mattresses and said, "Skinner, grab one of those and let's get moving."

I picked up the first one I saw and carried it down the hall on my back. They took me through some more doors and into the jail, then told me to find a bed and move in. There were ten individual cells, each with its own sliding bars for doors. The cells opened into a common area, which looked like a giant dog run. It held maybe three or four small tables for guys to sit around and play cards or checkers or chess. I must have looked pretty shook up, because the first guy I walked past said, "First time, huh?"

"Yeah, how did you know?"

"It's easy to recognize the first timers. Don't worry; we were all first timers once. Just a little advice, if I were you, I'd move into one of the cells down at this end. That other end'll be a bad neighborhood for you. You're the wrong color."

I thought, *What's he talking about? Both neighborhoods look crummy.* I shrugged my shoulders. *I guess prejudice is everywhere.*

He seemed like a nice enough guy, and maybe I should take his advice since I was about as lost as anyone could be. I threw my mattress on a bed and sat there for a while. I could hear some of the guys talking about me and making jokes about how I was new and how shook up I looked. I didn't care what they thought as long as they left me alone. I wasn't interested in impressing them. I was still in shock about being there in the first place.

After an hour or so, somebody called out, "Grub's here!"

I looked out my doorway and saw a guy walking along the outer bar perimeter of the dog run with trays of food. He began passing them through slots in the bars, just big enough for the trays. Everybody lined up, waiting to get a plate like a bunch of hungry animals. Somebody called out, "Hey Skinner, ain't you comin' out for your grub? Ya better get out here before somebody else grabs it."

I stood up to look and decided I didn't want anything. The "food" resembled warmed-up garbage.

"No thanks, I'm not hungry."

They all laughed.

"Don't like our food, hey?"

"He sounds real polite about it though, 'No thanks.'"

"Hey, I'm just not hungry."

"Yeah, that'll last another meal or two before you're up here beggin' for more like the rest of us."

I thought, *I'll starve first*.

I sat back down on my bed for a few minutes, still thinking about what I'd just gone through, wishing I could somehow wake up. I stared at the floor and the walls and the crummy toilet in the corner. It was very strange looking, actually, quite an invention. It was one piece with a toilet on the bottom and a sink on the top. There was no seat either. They wouldn't want us to have it too nice in here, would they?

The rest of the afternoon and evening went by slowly. There was literally nothing to do. I guess I could have started making friends or playing checkers or chess, but that all seemed repulsive. These guys were a bunch of convicts, and me, I didn't belong there. I was determined to not become like them. I did not fit in and I was not planning on making any efforts to either.

About this time a very large man stopped by my cell and stared at me. I didn't know what to do or say, so I stared back. Finally he broke the silence.

"Wanna lemon drop?"

"What?"

"A lemon drop."

He pulled out a box of lemon drop candy from his pocket and held it out for me to take some. Two things came to mind at the same time. First, I hated lemon drops. Second, this guy could break my neck in a heartbeat, so perhaps I should accept his gift and not tell him how I feel about lemon drops. I went with my second idea, and somewhat nervously, held out my hands. He poured a couple in and said, "The first day's the worst. Sometimes goodies can cheer a guy up."

"Thanks."

Then he smiled from ear to ear, and I couldn't help but notice about half his teeth were missing. That was another sign I didn't belong there. I had all my teeth.

Before he left he said one more thing.

"Just so you know, it's okay to cry in here. We all talk tough, but there ain't a one of us that ain't broke down 'n cried a few times. We're all pretty much sissy's without our guns and knives."

I didn't know what to say, so I just nodded. And that was all we said to each other. I was glad too, because I was sure to say something stupid if I continued the conversation. While I was touched by this small act of kindness, I wasn't interested in making any new friends—but I wasn't interested in making any enemies either.

I put the two lemon drops in my pocket, planning to throw them away later when I had the chance. The truth still remained: I hated lemon drops. Shortly after I heard one of the guards yell, "Lockdown, lockdown, lockdown!"

Within ten seconds the cell doors slammed shut, one at a time. "Kachunk, kachunk, kachunk, kachunk."

As I watched my door close my head started spinning. I thought, *This is the real deal, Skinner. It's not the movies and it's not a bad dream. You are a convicted felon and this is your new life.*

Since I had refused to eat lunch or supper because of the grossness of the food, a few hours later I felt hunger pangs. I thought, *Maybe those bologna sandwiches would've tasted all right after all. I sure am hungry now.*

Then I remembered the lemon drops. I popped one in my mouth.

"Hmmmm, lemon drops. Not so bad after all."

And that was the beginning of many events that, had they happened on the outside, I would have complained about, and grumbled how terrible things were. Since I was on the inside and it was tough to find things to be thankful for, some of the simplest pleasures became very special, like lemon drops.

I sat there for another hour or so. Even though it was late, I couldn't sleep. So many things ran through my mind. Since I had permission, I took it upon myself to do a little crying, quietly, but real tears and real sorrow, because this was real pain. I stood up and looked down at my new clothes. I remember what I said next as if it were yesterday.

"Well, Lord, I've really done it this time. I've really messed up about as bad as I could. I hate what I've done and I hate who I've become and I hate where I am. Lord, please don't let me die in here. Please don't let this be what I'm known for. Please don't let this be what my wife and kids think of when they think of me. Please don't let this be my legacy."

Then I sobbed pretty hard, feeling hopeless.

"Four to fifteen years in a state penitentiary..."

Those words just kept ringing in my head, over and over and over.

Chapter 16
Managing the New World

After I had been behind bars for a couple of days, I found myself standing in front of a mirror in my cell. Without thinking, I looked at my reflection and quietly sang, "I did it my way..."

This was somewhat funny, but not in a good way. The truth was I had done it my way, and doing things my way had really cost me. I found myself caught between wanting to laugh and wanting to cry.

I ended up living in the county jail for seven days before they transported me to a different facility. The county is a holding place for those going to trial and those waiting to be sent to their new homes after the trial. My next stop was a facility that looked a lot like a college campus, except for the razor wire around it. I found out later every criminal in the state went here for processing.

Everything was very strict and most of the time we were "locked down," which meant we were confined to our cells or an area in a large room marked off with tape on the floor. During lockdown no one in that particular area was allowed to step over the line, as it would have been considered as big a violation as breaking out of your cell.

For the first few days I shared a cell with a guy who had been transported from the county jail with me. He constantly cracked jokes and tried to make things seem better than they were. This was actually kind of refreshing, in spite of the fact that he was one of those guys who wouldn't shut up. He walked back and forth all day in our little cell as if perhaps he could wear a path through the concrete and escape.

After a week I was placed on "the floor" where the area was taped off. We were so crowded that they had us double bunked.

I didn't understand it at first, but the reason we were locked down all the time was because criminals of all types were there. Some were guys like me involved in "white-collar" crime; some were murderers and violent offenders; and of course some were petty thieves and drug offenders. This facility was like a "clearing house" for criminals until we were assigned to our permanent residence, where we would serve out our sentences. So the lockdown policy was actually for our own protection. This was also the place where we would get a physical exam to find out if we had any communicable diseases and some psychological testing to determination whether we were crazy or not. Knowing this, I was glad to be locked down, because I'd already seen a few who were easy to identify as lunatics without any testing.

Some guys preferred staying in a cell, but I was glad to get out. Although the common area had its limitations, it felt less restricting. I was at this facility for thirty-six days. They were some of the toughest days of all because I couldn't seem to adjust. A sense of hopelessness and depression permeated the atmosphere. Thoughts of condemnation were heavy. I often became overwhelmed with shame to the point that dying seemed like the best possible solution. No, I didn't consider killing myself, but more than once I thought things might be better off if I just died in my sleep. I slept a lot.

I began looking for some way to inspire some hope and fight off the condemnation. One of the most effective ways was reading the Bible, so I searched the Scriptures. I became so desperate that I didn't just read a couple of chapters a day; I read eight to ten hours a day, every day. In fact, I was either sleeping, eating or reading a Bible.

I read verse after verse after verse and didn't seem to get a thing out of it. I kept making myself read, but I didn't comprehend anything. It seemed as though some kind of war was going on in my head that was as critical as life and death. I thought to myself, *If I can just keep reading, even though I can't seem to concentrate, perhaps somewhere in this book, somewhere in these words I'll find life.*

Life is a strange thing. Prison was actually a step up for some of the guys. For me, however, I felt like I had reached the bottom of all humanity and that I had brought the worst ruin to my life possible.

For the next several weeks I dreamt almost every time I fell asleep. The dream was always the same. I was sitting in a restaurant with some friends and talking about what had happened with the business and how lucky I was not to have to go to prison. Then I would wake up and the reality of it all would drop like a brick into my heart. It took everything within me to keep from having an anxiety attack. I breathed in deeply, trying to calm myself. At other times, as I lay on my back staring at the ceiling, tears uncontrollably streamed down my face, yet I didn't feel like I was crying.

In retrospect, I do believe those days of reading the Scriptures gave me life and hope. It also brought me some respect from the guys and even the guards, though respect from anyone in there was the furthest thing from my mind. I wasn't aware of others most of the time. On a couple of occasions certain inmates tried to bully me. I would stop, look at them for a moment, then turn away and begin reading again. Once in a while a guy got offended at my response and said something. As soon as he said his remarks, another guy, somebody I didn't know, would speak up and say, "Hey, leave Skinner alone. He ain't botherin' nobody."

And then for whatever reason, the guy would walk away and leave me alone.

Before long I found ways to make my life a

little easier. Nothing major, just things like getting extra time on the phone or taking a shower more often than what was usually allowed. Inmates ran the prison. Yes, there were the guards, but they didn't do any of the work. Most of us were at this facility temporarily so we didn't do any work either. However, some guys who were there for a longer time were given responsibilities. Some even had a respectable level of authority. Each building or pod had one particular inmate who was assigned to manage things. The key man in our pod was Larry. Larry always talked tough and continually reminded us, "Nobody's gonna get any special treatment from me."

But that was nothing more than posturing in front of the guards. In reality he was afraid if he looked soft to them, perhaps he would be replaced. It didn't take long for me to figure out that getting a few extra freedoms from Larry was as simple as bringing him some "goodies" from the commissary. Twice a week we were allowed to go to the commissary—or "store" as the guys called it—to purchase pop, candy, chips, and other assorted "goodies." What and how much we purchased was determined by the amount of money we each had in our accounts. People from the outside could send in money, which was added to the books.

Well, I discovered what ol' Larry liked and bought it at the store. Then I'd take it back to the pod and drop it off at Larry's bed without saying a word. Sure enough, when it was my turn for a shower or phone time, he didn't pay any attention to the clock. In fact, he'd usually say, "Skinner, you take your time. There are other phones for the other guys. They can share."

In the beginning I thought the main reason Larry gave me such special treatment was because of the "goodies." I later found out Larry's mom was what he called "a prayin' Christian."

When Larry saw me reading the Bible, it reminded him of his mom and he wanted to take good care of me out of respect to her. It seemed like there wasn't a guy in the joint who didn't like their mom. Larry also noticed I treated everyone with respect, regardless of who they were. I wasn't wimpy about it; I just believed it was the least I could do. In my mind it didn't matter where I was or whom I was with, there was nothing to be gained by being disrespectful. In prison that kind of behavior seemed to stand out.

I also treated the guards with the same respect. Most of the guys looked at the guards as "them against us." I admit I thought the same way from time to time. But I acted toward them the same as I did the others. I didn't have a specific motivation; I just figured they were trying to do their jobs, and just because they were in charge of bossing us around didn't automatically make them rotten people. This attitude paid off in my favor more than once.

The most obvious incident happened just a few days before I was to be transferred to my permanent residence. It was in the middle of the afternoon and most of us were just taking a nap, when all of a sudden the main doors to the pod burst open, whistles blew and guards screamed, "Everybody...off your beds...right now!!"

They lined us up along the wall facing our beds, and one by one took everything we had and threw it on the floor. Even bedding was torn off. It was a huge mess. It was up to us inmates to find our stuff and put it all back and re-make our beds. Apparently the guards were looking for drugs or other "contraband" because a couple of the guys were handcuffed and taken away. A very interesting thing happened to me during this "shake down." When one guard came to my bed, another said, "That's Skinner's...leave it alone."

"But sir, I thought we were supposed to shake down everybody."

"Not this one...he's clean, leave him and his stuff alone!"

And he did. He went to the next bed. Not one other guy in the entire place got skipped over except me. This made me feel special for the moment, but after the guards left some of the guys complained, and one even confronted me.

"So, Skinner, who do you think you are?"

I didn't say anything. I just shrugged my shoulders, lay back on my bed, and started reading. Sure enough, just like always, one of the other guys spoke up and said, "Leave him alone. It's not his fault they decided to skip over him. He's not hurting you. Get over it!"

And he did.

Finally, my thirty-six days were up and I was going to move to my permanent residence. There was a lot of talk about how things would be when we got to our final destination, that prison life would be much better. Some of the guys who had been in before said we would have more access to television, more recreation, and more freedom to walk around. I thought it sounded better, but I didn't give the talk much credence. They were all a bunch of liars. After those thirty-six days I felt like I was getting a handle on my life and I would be able to manage things after all. Those feelings changed the moment I arrived at the "big house."

Chapter 17

Life in the Big House

They called it the "big house," and I'll never forget the day I moved there. About twenty of us went to the same prison. The guards got us up early and had us walk in single file to a rickety old bus that looked like something out of the 1950s.

Next they separated us into pairs, then handcuffed and leg ironed us together. It reminded me of some prison movies I had seen years ago. The entire day felt as though I was in some kind of black-and-white film because of how old everything was. The bus was old, the handcuffs were old, the leg irons were old, the guards were old, even the air seemed old.

We were not given a choice of "partners" for the day, so lucky me, I got a crazy little guy who wouldn't stand still. His head was shaved, several of his teeth were missing, and he rambled continually. I became really irritated. What bothered me the most was his insistence that he was planning an escape. He talked very fast and breathed very hard.

"Hey, ya know what I'm gonna do? (heavy breathing) "I'm gonna escape!" (heavy breathing)

At first I just looked at him.

"I done it before." (heavy breathing) "I can do it again." (heavy breathing)

Then he looked at me and smiled, his black teeth showing, and continued his heavy breathing.

"Yep, I'm gonna do it, I'm gonna escape!" (heavy breathing) "I gotta plan and I'm gonna do it!" (heavy breathing)

Finally, I had enough of his ranting and decided to set him straight.

"No, you're not, buddy! As long as you're chained to me, you're going to do exactly what you are supposed to do."

"No, I'm not, I'm gonna escape!" (big smile, heavy breathing)

"Look at your hands, they are chained to me. Look at your feet, they are chained to me. You are not going anywhere except where I am going. I am not escaping and neither are you, so just get it out of your mind. In fact, if you even try to make a move I'll choke your head off."

I'm not the violent type and this was not a typical response for me, but I needed to say something to get this guy's attention. There was no doubt in my mind that if he tried anything strange, these old guards would not hesitate to take us both out with their shotguns.

He must have gotten the message because he stopped talking to me. He just turned his head toward the window and pressed his nose against the glass for the rest of the trip. Every once in a while I heard him whisper to himself, "I'm gonna escape, I'm gonna escape, I'm gonna escape."

I wasn't concerned. It was just annoying. I was certainly looking forward to being separated from my new friend.

As the bus pulled into the long lane that led up to the "big house," a shudder ran through my body. I had just spent the last thirty-six days in a brand-new facility and for some reason had thought my new permanent housing would look the same. I was wrong. This was something out of the early 1900s, very old, and very depressing. My heart sank.

We got off the bus. The guards removed our cuffs and leg irons and marched us down a long corridor to the basement. It smelled rotten, it looked rotten, and I wondered if the ceiling might cave in on us. A guard gave us a short orientation speech, then told us to grab a locker box and head up to our rooms. I assumed my room would be a cell with maybe two or three other guys in it. Instead, we were taken to these huge rooms that each housed about a hundred and eighty men. One of the guards walked me to my bed and pointed to my name and number taped to the top of the metal frame.

"Skinner 247-195."

It seemed so cold and impersonal. I had been given a new identity. It had a degrading feel to it. Of course, nobody said prison was supposed to be an uplifting experience.

The room was noisy, and smoky. It was as if there were no rules whatsoever, just a big free-for-all. I had just come from a facility that required complete silence, and smoking was not allowed. This was not an easy transition. The noise level was incredible. The next time you go to a professional baseball or football game, walk into the hallway where the concessions are, stop for a moment, and listen. It is nothing but a continuous roar. You cannot make out what anyone is saying and it sounds like everybody is talking a lot louder than necessary. That is exactly what it was like in those dorm rooms. It would start up around seven o'clock in the morning and continue throughout the day until about 11:00 at night. This continued day after day, week after week, month after month. I thought I would get used to it eventually, but I never did. I made it a point to wake myself up in the middle of the night just so I could sit and listen to silence for a while.

I never got used to the smoking either. For some of these guys, smoking cigarette after cigarette was the only thing they could think of to do.

After about two hours had passed, a voice over the intercom called out, "Count-time, count-time."

During this procedure, everyone had to be on their beds, or as some would say, "In their house." Each "house" consisted of a bed and two feet of space on one side where we were allowed to store a small locker box. We were also a part of a "neighborhood," which consisted of the few beds closest to you. The penitentiary did not designate us in neighborhoods, but we did. The sizes varied, as they were determined by demographics. There were the young neighborhoods, the old neighborhoods, the loud neighborhoods, and the quiet neighborhoods. They became what they were by those who dominated the area. I was fortunate to be assigned to an older, quieter neighborhood.

Some neighborhoods were not pleasant. Fights often broke out and if a guy was living in that area, he might get caught right in the middle of something. Thankfully, most of the guys in my area kept to themselves. In fact, the inmate on my left didn't say a word to me for the first three months. His bed was the only one without a number on it. The tag taped on his bed frame simply said, "Blood." That was all I needed to make sure I didn't annoy him. I overheard him talking to other guys, but he never said a word to me, so I never said a word to him.

Actually, that was a part of my survival strategy. I never started a conversation. I didn't try to make friends. I just kept to myself. My theory was if I didn't talk much, I couldn't say much wrong to offend anyone. Some of the guys talked all the time, going from neighborhood to neighborhood as if they were running for office. Many of the "new" guys talked to everyone, trying to fit in, and sure enough, eventually they said something insulting. Then the pushing and shoving started, until an all out fist fight erupted. I didn't need the grief.

There was no shortage of bullies in my new society of friends. I was only on the premises about ten hours before I was given the opportunity to deal with one such personality.

I was quietly minding my own business when this very large, loud, intimidating gorilla of a man decided to "front" me. That is what they called it when somebody tried to test you. It went like this: A bully would get in the mood to pick a fight. He would rarely have a good reason; he was just in the mood. He would either find someone about half his size who looked easy to intimidate, or someone new to the dorm. The bully would loudly call the guy out to see how he would react. They all referred to this as being "called out on Front Street."

It was a crummy situation to be caught in. If a guy didn't fight the bully, he was labeled a coward and life became miserable. He was "marked." Whenever a bully was in the mood to push somebody around, he looked for one of these "marked" guys to take advantage of. This was very bad news for me because I was not experienced in the skills of self-defense, nor was I one to participate in such nonsense. To make things worse, I was half the size of about eighty percent of the guys in the room, so I knew I'd be a prime target if things didn't go well with this first confrontation. Of course, I wasn't thinking this thoroughly at the time; I was just dealing with the moment.

The guy walked up to my bed and yelled, "Skinner! Loan me some chips!"

I was startled and quickly sat up.

"I'm sorry, what did you say?"

I wasn't really sorry, and I was pretty sure that I knew what he had said, but stalling seemed like a good thing to do.

He blurted out even louder, "I said, loan me some chips!"

The room was quiet and all eyes were on us. Normally, if we had been out on the street somewhere, I would have just given him the chips. It was not a big deal. They were just potato chips. But we were not out on the street somewhere, we were in the "big house," and this request was a setup. If I didn't loan him the chips, he would start a fight. If I did loan him the chips, every moocher in the joint would stop by every day to borrow something. In the midst of my stalling, I got an idea.

I stood up and looked him right in the eye. By now a crowd had formed around us, hoping for a fight. The outcome was predictable because of my size, but these kinds of things never mattered to the guys. They just liked the excitement, even if it was going to be a quick slaughter.

I began to talk loudly so everyone could hear.

"You know, I would love to loan you some chips, but I can't. You see I've got this rule. I don't borrow anything from anybody and I don't loan anything to anybody. If I were to loan you the chips, I'd be breaking my own rule, and then I couldn't respect myself any longer. And as you know, in this place, a guy has got to keep at least a little respect for himself. I'm really sorry, but I just can't do it."

Well, to my surprise, he bought it. He took a couple of steps back and said, "Ya know Skinner,

I respect that. You're all right."

Then he really surprised me. He stuck out his hand. We shook hands, and that was the last time anyone ever "fronted" me again. Now it might have been on certain bullies' minds to try their skills at "fronting" me, but another event put those thoughts to rest.

Ironically, the success of my future security occurred as the result of me breaking my own rule of "no loans." Late one night I heard a guy call, "Hey, Skinna, loan me ya headphones!"

I looked over my shoulder. It was the last person in the world I wanted to ask me anything. It was Big Dave, the biggest, toughest, strongest, and meanest guy in the dorm. He was loud and he was strong and he wasn't afraid of anyone. I did not want to be fronted by this guy. The good news is he wasn't really trying to front me; he just wanted to borrow my headphones.

"Sorry, Dave, but you know about my rule. I just can't."

"Aw, come on Skinna, please? I just wanna borrow 'em when you're not usin' 'em, you know, late at night, after you're asleep. I have trouble sleepin', so if I could listen to some music on your headphones, well, it would help me get through my time here. I promise I'll bring 'em back every morning and lay 'em nicely on your locker box. Please?"

This was not a guy trying to take advantage of me. This was Big Dave, a tough guy who was talking softly and respectfully to somebody he could smear all over the floor if he chose to. I caved.

"Okay, Dave, but they've got to be back here on my locker box in the morning just like you said or it will be the last time."

"Thanks, Skinna."

He ran over to my house and I handed him the headphones. Then he went back to his house, stood up on his bed, and yelled to get everyone's attention.

"Hey everybody, look over here. Right now, stop what you're doin' and listen to me! You see that guy over there? That's Skinna. Skinna's my nigga'. This announcement is to put everybody on notice that anybody who messes with Skinna messes with me!"

At first I didn't know what to think.

Was that a compliment?

I thought, *I'm not his nigga...at least I don't think I am...I wonder what that means? I don't think I'll ask.*

I felt more than a little silly, but later it was actually comforting to know I had a bodyguard. The entire time I was there, I felt like I was living in a protective bubble. The peace of God continually enveloped me, and I always had a sense that He was taking care of me. This little antic by Big Dave was, in a sense, a confirmation to let me know I was safe in the big house.

Several funny things happened between Big Dave and I over the next several months. One incident in particular will give you a flavor of just how influential Big Dave was in our dorm. I was sitting on a bench by the pay phones with several other guys, waiting my turn to call home. I had been sitting there for about fifteen minutes, biding my time, minding my own business. All of a sudden, Big Dave walked around the corner and looked my way.

"Hey, Skinna, are you waitin' for a phone?"

"Yeah."

"Well, you shouldn't have to wait. Let me help you out."

"No, Dave, it's fine, I'll wait my turn. Besides, it wouldn't be fair."

"Now Skinna, why don't you let me be the judge of what's fair around here?"

The next thing I knew, he walked over to one of the guys who was talking on the phone and interrupted him.

"Hey buddy, get off the phone!"

The guy looked at Dave, turned away, and just kept talking.

"Hey, can't you hear? I said, get off the phone!"

"I'm talkin' to my girlfriend. Get in line like everybody else." Then he turned his back on Dave again.

Dave grabbed the guy by the shoulders.

"I said, get off the phone!"

The guy put the phone up against his chest to muffle the conversation and said, "Can't you see I'm talkin' on the phone? Sit down and wait your turn."

Big mistake.

Dave ripped the phone out of the guy's hand, slammed it down, picked the guy up by the front of his shirt, and literally threw him about ten feet across the room, where he crashed into the side of a bed. The guy looked furious, but scared. All of a sudden he came to his senses and realized whom he was arguing with. He whispered something under his breath and walked away. Dave just stood there looking at me with a big cheesy grin on his face. Then he made a gesture with his left arm as if he were presenting me with an award. He spoke in a soft and gentlemanly manner, "Skinna, the phone."

I felt more than a little uncomfortable as everyone's eyes were glued to me to see how I would react. It was not a good time to give Big Dave an education on courtesy, so I did what he asked. I stepped up to the phone and accepted his offering.

"Thanks, Dave, but I could have waited my turn and been just fine."

I had no idea at the time what an impact that incident had on the rest of the dorm. Dave made it clear he was prepared to back up his words with action, and that what he had said about me being his friend was not to be taken lightly. More than once I faced situations where the outcome could have been less than desirable, yet because of the reputation of being Dave's friend, I was spared the trouble.

Some of the guys, had they been in the same

situation as myself, might have tried to take advantage of Big Dave's friendship. I chose to let it be what it was. Actually, I wasn't much of a friend to him. I didn't spend time with him or talk to him very often. The only thing I did was loan him my headphones every night, and only after I was finished with them.

It's interesting to me how important it was not to cave in on the "chips" incident, and how equally important it was to agree to loan Dave my headphones. If I had gotten those two incidents turned around, I would have been in a fight every other day, and Big Dave would have just taken my headphones and harassed me like he did everybody else. Some of you might think I was just "lucky," but the truth is I got some divine help by listening to that inner voice for wisdom and direction in critical moments. I did not know how to hear from God very well, but He always seemed to be there when I got in a tough circumstance. I think God directed my relationship with "Blood" in the same manner.

"Blood" wasn't as big or as strong as Dave, but the steely look in his eyes told me he wouldn't hesitate to break a guy's neck if the occasion presented itself. After a few months had passed, I assumed I would never get to know him. One night, however, as I was lying down, reading a book, I felt a tapping on the side of my bed. I rolled over and there was Blood staring at me. He wasn't smiling or looking as if he wanted to strike up a conversation. At first I thought I'd made a mistake by rolling over. All of a sudden, he held out a snack bag and said, "Want some hot fries?"

I thought, *I hate hot fries.*

But then I remembered my first day in the county jail and the incident with the lemon drops. So I said, "Yeah, sure, thanks."

He smiled and said, "Skinner, I've been watchin' you and you're all right. If you need anything, you just let me know and I'll help you out."

"Yeah, sure, thanks."

That was the longest conversation we ever had. But we did become pretty good silent friends. I knew he was there if I needed him and he knew I wasn't going to bother him with a lot of small talk.

The fact is, I did end up making several "once in a while" friends, who respected me and let me know that if I ever needed them, they were there for me. In a place like this it didn't hurt to have a few guys on my side.

Chapter 18

Bounced Around

It might seem as though I was doing well for myself, but actually, I wasn't doing well at all. With regard to my family, the people I loved the most, I was absolutely powerless to help with anything. When I wrote letters or talked to them on the phone, I tried to find the right words to comfort or encourage, but my words seldom helped. I recall Susan talking to me about things she had to deal with on the outside. She had to move twice, work with creditors, find money to live on, and raise Todd by herself. Sure, I had my problems on the inside, but in many ways Susan had it more difficult.

After almost every phone call I went back to my "house" feeling like the biggest loser of all time. Often I lay down on my bed, wrapped a towel around my head, and prayed. Whenever a guy put a towel around his head, it meant he wanted some space, some solitude. The inmates always respected that. My prayers seemed to end up sounding the same. "Lord, you know my situation. You know I am unable to do anything from here. I trust You, and so once again, I give Susan and Todd to You. I'm trusting You to take care of their needs and to get them through this time."

Some of you might think this was a lazy way to handle things, but the truth of the matter was, there wasn't anything else I *could* do. This really taught me about having faith in God. The way I saw it there were only two choices. I could worry, complain, and whine about how terrible life was for my family, or I could trust God. I saw Him work a lot of miracles through that time. Because of those experiences, I am able to release problems to him now with confidence. I really do trust Him. Let's face it, He's more powerful, more wise, more everything.

After a month in the big house my daily routine began to set in. I got three meals a day and plenty of sleep. Sometimes the only solace for depression was to take a nap. I continued to read the Bible, but more as a daily lifestyle rather than out of desperation. I spent much of my time conversing with God, though I didn't have the sense that He was saying much to me. Unfortunately, most of my prayers had more to do with me getting out than anything else. It was all I could think about.

About this time I found out I qualified to apply for "shock probation." I had to fill out some paperwork and file it with the courts so the judge who sentenced me could review my case. The judge had sixty days to respond. If approved, I would be released on probation for five years. I wasn't too concerned about the terms of my release; I just wanted to go home.

On the sixtieth day I received my answer.

"Rejected."

That was a tough day. The "four to fifteen" started looking more and more like "fifteen" than it did "four." A few weeks after my rejection, I found that I was eligible to apply for "shock parole." It would mean going before the parole board rather than the judge. The board was more likely to give a guy a break because of the overcrowding. Releasing inmates who weren't a threat to society provided more room for locking up serious offenders. The big house was originally designed to hold 900 inmates. It currently had over 2,400. Since my crime was non-violent and non-threatening to society, I was in fair shape to get a break. If they awarded me "shock parole" I would be released sixty days after the decision, remain on parole for one year, and then be able to go about my life in a normal manner.

By the time I was granted a hearing and brought before the parole board for an interview, I had already done six months of my sentence. It seemed much longer.

Once a month the parole board visited each of the prisons for a couple of days. The board had eleven members. They divided up into panels of two or three and met in separate rooms with parole candidates. My panel consisted of two men. They sat behind a small table, while I sat in a chair in the middle of the room. They asked me a variety of generic questions like, "Do you believe you have learned your lesson?" and "Why do you believe you will never commit another crime?"

Then they asked specific questions regarding my case. I thought it was going pretty well until all of a sudden they stopped and looked at each other. They got up and one of them said, "We'll be right back. This is more complicated than we thought."

They left the room. I hoped and prayed I'd get a break and be able to go home. They came back in about five minutes, walked over to their chairs, and sat down. The spokesman of the two said, "Mr. Skinner, due to the complexity of your case we are not able to make a clear judgment today concerning your request for shock parole. We recommend therefore, that you have a full board review so the proper judgment can be determined."

"What exactly does that mean?"

"It means you need to meet with the entire board and explain the details of your case. Then we will collectively make a decision."

"Okay, whatever is necessary. What do I need to do?"

"You need to come back next month."

"Oh, we don't need to wait until next month. I'm ready now."

"That may be true, Mr. Skinner, but we are not prepared to meet with you at this time. We'll see you again in thirty days."

"Thirty days, why so long?"

"Mr. Skinner, thirty days is not so long, and you are dismissed."

Well, I knew I'd better shut up before they got angry, so I thanked them for their time and left.

I couldn't help but think they were out of touch with reality. Thirty days was forever in my mind. I guess that's one of the big differences about being locked up with nothing but time on your hands and being on the outside where it seems there is never enough. Time was such a rotten, lonely thing on the inside. Days seemed like weeks, weeks seemed like months, and months seemed like years. A large part of the problem was that there wasn't anything to do all day. It would have been better to have a crummy job than no job, but there weren't enough to go around. I tried to control my mind, but it was a struggle. I was constantly barraged with thoughts of going home, thoughts of condemnation and shame, and thoughts of anger toward the people I viewed as responsible for me getting locked up.

I started asking some of the guys about this "full board review." Instead of answering, they asked me questions.

"What kind of crime did you commit anyway?"

"The only time there is a full board review is for a high profile case like a murder or something big."

Mine was considered a high profile case because of the amount of money involved. Supposedly anything over $100,000 was considered serious. The guys tried to encourage me.

"Hey, it must be good news, otherwise they'd a just turned you down on the spot."

And actually that was kind of encouraging.

It seemed like a lot longer than thirty days, but finally the big day arrived. I walked into the room and sat down in front of all eleven parole board members. I brought a lot of paperwork to help me back up my answers. I was prepared to go through everything step by step if necessary. I decided ahead of time there was no point in trying to convince them that what I had done was not that bad. I felt my only chance was for the board to see that I was remorseful and desired to make everything right.

The meeting lasted about a half an hour. They seemed to be pleased with most of my answers. I had been in sales for so many years that I could almost always tell when someone agreed with me. In this case I only needed six out of the eleven to go my way. As I looked around the room I felt confident at least that many were with me. Something else is important to mention: A board member named Mrs. Jackson kept coming to my aide. If I had trouble communicating what I was trying to say, she spoke up and helped me out. I will admit I was quite nervous since so much was riding on their approval.

Finally, they asked me to leave the room while they voted. I was only in the hallway for two or three minutes before they invited me back in.

The parole board president spoke up. "Mr. Skinner, we've decided to grant you shock parole. There is a processing period for all parolees of sixty days, so you will be going home two months from today. Congratulations."

I was ecstatic. Gary was going home. I was so excited I could hardly stand it. All of a sudden, sixty days didn't seem that long at all. I was going home.

Those next couple of months were somehow a lot more fun than the previous ones. I started making all kinds of plans about where I would work, and thinking how great it would be to see Susan and Todd and the rest of my family and friends. Even though some of the reunions would be a little uncomfortable, I just knew all would be fine in time. I must have thanked God a million times over the next few weeks. I even made a chart with sixty days on it and crossed off the days one at a time. It was almost as if I were already free.

Three days before I was supposed to go home, I was lying on my bed and a guard stopped by to hand me a letter. It was from the parole board. I opened it and couldn't believe my eyes. They said they wanted to review my case one more time. I was to meet with them in thirty days.

"No, this can't be right. What's going on?"

I started asking, but no one had a clue, not the inmates, not the guards. They tried to be nice. "Aw, don't worry about it. It's probably some technicality they want to clear up. You haven't done anything wrong. It's a little delay, but nothin' to worry about."

I wanted to be optimistic, but no matter how

hard I tried, I couldn't get rid of a sick feeling in the pit of my stomach that seemed to scream, "Skinner, you're never going to get out of this place!"

Those next thirty days seemed like years. I was a nervous wreck. Finally the day arrived and I walked into that room again. They were all there, all eleven of them, just like before. Something was wrong this time. I couldn't put my finger on it, but I sensed something drastic had changed since the last time we met. I sat down and they started all over again, asking me the same questions as before. I gave them the same answers, but it didn't seem like it was going as well. The parole board president appeared very upset with me. He kept drilling me with question after question as if he were trying to trap me in my own words. It was to no avail. I was telling the truth.

As he continued I started to get a little hopeful, because it was obvious the decision they made the first time was the right decision. After twenty minutes they asked me to leave the room. I waited fifteen minutes before they called me back in. Once again, the president didn't waste any time.

"Mr. Skinner, after much consideration, we have decided to revoke your parole."

I couldn't believe my ears. This had to be a dream, a very, very bad dream. I looked at each board member one by one, hoping for some help. As my eyes moved from person to person, they dropped their heads or looked away or stared at the table in front of them. I thought, *What happened to my votes? They have still got to be in this room. They were here three months ago; they've still got to be here.*

I stared at Mrs. Jackson, my eyes imploring her to help. She was on my side for sure. But she looked away just like the others. Only two didn't look away: an older lady and the president. I tried very hard to keep my cool.

"May I ask a question?"

"Yes, Mr. Skinner, you may."

"What happened? Why was I okay three months ago and now I'm not? What did I do wrong? I've been a model prisoner since the day I was sentenced. I've followed every rule. I have been honorable toward every person I've been in contact with. I have done nothing but treat everyone—including the guards, the staff, and all of you—with the utmost respect. Three months ago you said I was approved. You said I could go home. Please tell me what I've done wrong. Please tell me what happened!"

"We've changed our minds, that's all."

The older lady spoke up. "You'll be fine, Mr. Skinner. We'll review you again in two years."

"Two years! Two years?!"

"Yes, we'll see you again in two years."

She said it with such enthusiasm, as if she were giving me some really great news. I wanted to die.

The silence was deafening. I didn't know what

else to say or do, so as calmly and politely as I could I said, "May I please be excused?"

"Yes, Mr. Skinner, you can go now."

I turned and walked out of the room, totally confused, devastated, and broken. My head began to throb. It was as if the halls were spinning and I could hardly walk straight. It suddenly felt as though someone had sucked all the air out of my lungs.

"What am I going to tell Susan?"

Chapter 19

A Very Good Decision

It took me awhile to get my composure. I sat down on the bench to wait my turn for a phone. Part of me wanted to get it over with, and part of me didn't want to make the call at all. After about ten minutes one of the phones opened up. I called Susan and blurted it out. "They took it away. I lost my parole."

After thirty seconds of silence, she said, "I can't talk now. I've got to go."

Click.

That dial tone was the loneliest sound ever.

I walked out of the dorm and downstairs to the yard, the only place where I could be somewhat alone. Probably a hundred or so other guys were there, but at least I was outside and could walk around by myself.

It was strange really. They called it "the yard" but there wasn't any grass. It was just a big blacktop area between two buildings with razor wire surrounding it. Inmates went there for recreation, i.e. walking outside.

I stood near a corner of a building by myself. My head kept throbbing. I wanted to throw up, but I was too sick to throw up. All my energy drained from my body. This by far was the worst day of my life, even worse than the day I was sentenced. You see, I had already lost so much by then, the house and the cars and my reputation. I had disgraced my family and myself, and up until now, I still had my family. Now I wasn't confident that I'd be able to keep them. I felt completely alone that day.

Even though the board said they would review me again in two years, no promises were made. I already knew of a guy who had done five years for a similar crime and the board had just given him another two. What kept pressing on my mind was the possibility I might have to do the entire fifteen years. I started adding up how old I would be. To make it worse, my mind continued to replay Susan's words over and over and the sound of that lonely dial tone after she hung up.

It happened every week. Some poor joker would get the paperwork in the mail and find out he was being divorced. It was so common that down deep, nobody really believed they would get home before they received those papers. Well, nobody but me. I was sure, that no matter what, Susan would wait it out. I wasn't so sure that day. Something about that phone call sucked away my hopes, and I wasn't in any state of mind to blame her.

This new twist changed everything inside of me. I felt like I had lost my wife, my family, and any hope of a reasonable future all in one fell swoop. For the first time in my life, I felt abandoned by all. It even seemed like God had turned away from me. I cannot describe my emptiness. I looked at the sky and started talking to God. I wasn't angry and I didn't get loud. In fact, I spoke in an almost apologetic tone.

"Lord...where are You? It feels like You are a million miles away. I know You've got to be here because Your Word says You never leave us. But it feels like You have left me. Am I going to lose Susan? Am I going to lose my family? It feels like they are already gone. It feels like I'm going to die in here...alone."

I stood in silence for a couple of minutes. Then something came out of my mouth—and I don't know how, because it was as if I said it without thinking about it. "Lord...I just want You to know that if it comes down to just You and me, it's okay. If I end up losing everyone and end up dying in here, it's okay. It's not what I want, but if all I have for the rest of my life is You, it's okay."

Then I began a prayer of thanks. I don't know where it came from because I didn't feel thankful. I don't know why or how I was able to be thankful, but gratitude started pouring out of me. I stood there looking at the sky, and then I took a breath. "Thank You, Lord, that I can breathe."

Then I took a step. "Thank You, Lord, that I can walk."

I raised my hands. "Thank You, Lord, that I can move my arms. Thank You for all You've done for me. Thank You for sending Your Son. Thank You for Your goodness and mercy."

It kept pouring out of my mouth, almost uncontrollably. I began thanking Him for everything. "Thank You for birds. Lord, thank You for flowers and trees and concrete, and bricks and blacktop and razor wire."

It didn't seem to matter how ridiculous the thought, everything turned into some kind of exuberant thankfulness. It continued for about ten minutes as I stood there with tears streaming down my face. Despite this gratitude, I did not feel comforted. It was a very strange moment. I would like to say that in the midst of this dramatic experience I felt the warm arms of my Heavenly Father surround and comfort me, but I didn't. I would like to say I had a sense of God looking down upon me with eyes of favor, but I didn't. I didn't feel anything. I didn't hear anything. I didn't sense anything. Nothing. Just emptiness. It felt as though God was on the other side of the world somewhere, too far away to hear me, too busy to care.

After I regained my composure, I walked back to the dorm, lay down on my bed, wrapped a towel around my head, and embraced my numbness. As terrible as everything felt, I knew deep within me that I had just responded perfectly to my circumstances. Something changed that day between God and I, in a very good way. Although I had much to work on and change in my life, I knew something special was going on. My heart went to a new depth of knowing Him that I could not explain then or now.

I believe for a person to get close to God in an intimate way, he has to make the same decision and choice I did that day.

"If it's just You and me, Lord, it's okay."

I'm not saying everyone has to go to prison or go through some horrible life experience to make such a decision, but nonetheless, if you haven't made it, you need to if you really want to know Him deeply. You see, when you make that decision, you are proving you love Him more than anything or anyone or even life itself. God is very loving, yet He is also very jealous. He wants every part of us, not just what we have left at the end of the day. This is the kind of mettle martyrs are made of. This is how a person can live for God and not be shaken in his faith. It is how a person gets to the place of being sold out, committed, unwavering. Before that day I didn't understand how a person could attain such a level of faith. Since that day I've never forgotten. I was changed forever.

Chapter 20

Not So Safe Anymore

Over the next few weeks I began to change how I managed my life. I realized I could not continue to mentally approach things the way I'd been doing. I needed to embrace where I was and eliminate the thoughts of "I'm getting out of here soon." Because the truth was, I wasn't.

I had been calling Susan four to five times a week. I dumped all my struggles on her and she dumped all her struggles on me. In effect we were trying to live in each other's world. This was ridiculous because it was impossible to achieve. It just caused me to resent my situation all the more, and resent those I believed responsible for sending me to prison.

My encounter with God in the yard helped me accept that I wasn't going home in the near future. I also realized I needed to live a life of thankfulness, regardless of my circumstances. These conclusions seemed to help me to grow in a new sense of confidence. It was as though I gained clarity and direction. I came up with some guidelines.

"Susan, I have to stop calling you so frequently. Beginning immediately, I will call you only once a week. I have to learn how to live in here without you, and you have to learn how to live out there without me. I have to trust God for my comfort and encouragement, and you have to trust God for your needs, both materially and emotionally."

As tough as it was to have that conversation, it proved a huge breakthrough for both of us. It forced us to focus on His guidance instead of our own ideas and plans.

At first, reducing my contact with Susan was difficult, especially since communication with friends and family had gradually decreased. In the beginning I received four to five letters a week from different people. By now I got one letter every other week. With one exception, visitations followed suit.

Initially a couple of friends were pretty good about stopping by. Yet the longer I was inside, the more awkward those visits became. It was a hassle for my friends to get through the security checks, and I was running out of things to talk about. Life in prison is very mundane. There aren't too many ways to make eating and sleeping exciting topics.

Susan lived several hundred miles away in another state, so she was unavailable most of the time. The champion visitors were my parents. They faithfully drove several hours both ways to see me every two weeks without fail. The great thing was we didn't have to talk about much of anything, we were just happy to look at each other. Sometime during those visits my Dad and I began to close the distance I had created between us over the years.

Both Mom and Dad were amazing. They never once condemned me. I think their response allowed me to receive forgiveness from God and eventually forgive myself. It was as though they could see past my prison garb and my deplorable circumstances. They still believed in me.

Awhile after establishing new guidelines with Susan, I made a friend named "Doc." He was an older man, extremely intelligent and kind. Doc was the head clerk in the gym and ten months into my sentence, I was fortunate enough to be assigned as his assistant. We had some great conversations; he was somebody I could trust. Whatever the reason for his imprisonment, it was clear from our conversations that God had done a great work in his life. He had an uncanny ability to see the good in almost every situation and became a great encourager to me.

I'll never forget one Friday evening when the gym was packed. For some reason, the gym seemed to attract a large crowd on the weekends. It often became too crowded to play basketball or participate in any serious exercise. Guys would just stand around and talk, very loudly, for hours. Doc hated to be in the gym on Friday nights. Since I was his assistant, it became my automatic duty to sit in the office those evenings. My primary role was to answer questions about tournament schedules.

The evening was about half over and I was already counting the minutes before I could close up and go back to the dorm. All of a sudden there was a knock on the door. I looked up and it was Doc. I spoke to him in a joking manner, "What are you doing here? You hate to come here on Fridays. Are you confused or lost?"

"No, Gary, I'm here on purpose."

"What in the world for? It must be something really important for you to force yourself to come up here tonight."

"Well, as a matter of fact, it is something really important."

He stretched out his arm, opened his hand, and laid a small bag of peanut M&Ms on my desk.

"I know it's not much, but happy birthday, Gary."

Then he smiled and walked right back out the door.

I sat there for a moment and just stared at those M&Ms. A couple of tears fell down my face. I felt overwhelmed by his act of kindness. Yes, it was my birthday. I had forgotten. Actually, everybody had forgotten. My wife, my family, my friends—nobody had sent me a card. Since I hadn't remembered, I wasn't bothered by their forgetfulness. Yet in the midst of the deafening noise of that gym, at a time when I was separated from everyone I loved, a convicted felon who barely knew me took the time and effort to bring me a present. He could have waited until Monday when the gym was quieter. He could have given it to me on Thursday in advance. No, he waited until the day and the time that would mean the most. Sometimes Jesus shows up in the most unlikely ways.

I thought, "Too bad I don't like peanut M&Ms; it could have been perfect."

Of course I ate them with pleasure. It's like lemon drops and hot fries. They don't have to taste good. They just have to be eaten.

It was a great reminder that no matter who we are and no matter what our circumstances, a kind word or a small gift goes a long way in making the unbearable better. In a way, it was a sign that God was still paying attention to me. He knew everyone would forget my birthday. Yet He found a willing accomplice to carry out His will for that moment to make His point.

God has always had His ways of letting me know He's around. Sometimes it's obvious through gestures like I had just experienced with Doc, while other times He has worked in unseen, unheard, often unnoticed ways. For example, I never once in prison felt like my life was in danger, even in the presence of some potentially dangerous circumstances and some dangerous men. I felt so safe I hardly ever thought about being otherwise.

I do remember, however, the day all of that changed. It was almost as if someone lowered the walls of protection that I had taken for granted.

The actual event was something totally unrelated to me personally. It took place during our recreation time in the early evening. We were all out in the yard, some lifting weights, some standing around, others of us walking and talking about what we had for supper or some other insignificant blather. All of a sudden we heard the intercom come on and a voice announce, "Clear the yard, clear the yard, everyone off the yard. Clear the yard, clear the yard, everyone off the yard."

This was unusual in that we still had about an hour left on our recreation time. We all knew exactly what to do: Go to our dorms and wait for further instructions. As we filed into the building I noticed a crowd of guards hovering over one inmate in the corner. I could see the man's body convulsing as blood spurted out of his neck. One of the gangs had gotten to him.

There were several gangs in the prison and they were nothing to be messing with. Most of the time, I didn't think about them. As long as you stayed in your world and out of theirs, they hardly ever got involved in your business. The best way to stay out of their world was to not join them, steer away from drugs, and avoid gambling. If a guy joined a gang, it was just a matter of time before he would have to defend himself physically. If a guy was involved in drugs, it was just a matter of time before something went bad with a deal. If a guy was involved in gambling, it was just a matter of time before he got himself in trouble with a payoff.

I didn't know the inmate who was bleeding, nor did I have any reason to fear for myself. But now I didn't feel as safe as I used to. Maybe it was because I'd never seen someone hurt so badly. Perhaps it was because Big Dave had been released to go home a few days prior. It also might have been because I realized I was going to be living there for a long time, and I was becoming more sensitive to the reality of my environment. Whatever the reason, the climate of safety had changed.

I followed the congestion of men pushing their way back into the main building and went to my dorm. I laid down on my bed and thought about what I had just seen.

What a horrible thing. I wonder what he did to get himself into that situation? Whatever it was, it is a good reminder to keep to myself and choose my friends wisely.

The evening settled in and nobody talked about it much. There were the common opinions of "a gang got him," but no details of why. I thought it was a good time to have a little heart-to-heart talk with God.

"Lord, something has changed around here. I know You are here with me, but I don't have the same sense of safety that I've had up to this point. If there is any way You could work it for me to be transferred 'out back,' I sure would appreciate it."

"Out back" referred to the honor camp, or farm, one mile behind the main prison. Those who had graduated through the system lived out their time at the camp, which offered a more positive environment. Everyone there worked a full-time, manual labor job. Plus the food didn't have dirt in it, there were more choices at meals, and they even had condiments. Nothing like a little ketchup and mustard to make some of those sandwiches go down easier. The dorms were quiet and less crowded, and smoking was not allowed inside. There were no fences or razor wire. It was like being on the outside except for the inmates' attire and obvious prison limitations. There was a lot of talk about how good it was "out back," but there was no way to arrange for a transfer until the system was ready to send you there.

I didn't know for sure what I was asking for when I prayed that prayer, except I was confident life was better and safer "out back." I rolled over after that prayer and fell asleep. The next thing I realized, it was morning and time for me to get up to start my day. Before I could get myself fully awake, one of the guards slapped the top of my bed frame and said, "Hey, Skinner...pack your stuff, you're goin' 'out back.' "

That's what I call a quick answer. I didn't hesitate. I gathered my things and followed him to a group of other guys who were waiting to board the prison bus and head off to our new quarters. It felt strange to ride the bus away from the fences and razor wire. Although it was a very short ride, it felt good to graduate. It sparked a fresh hope in me.

Maybe I will get out of this place someday.

The camp was cleaner, quieter, and much

more pleasant than any of the guys had described. No more choking on other people's smoke. No more screaming guards and loud arguments. The food was much better. Everything was much better. Even the guards were different, which was odd, because many of them were the same guards who had worked "inside." They not only treated us with more respect, but they lent us a hand with carrying heavy loads. At meals it was common for them to actually sit and talk to us.

I'll never forget my first day at my new job. I had been assigned to the dairy barn and my duties were to help a crew of men milk a couple hundred cows every morning. We had to get up at 4:30 to be driven to the barn. I remember riding in the back of a pickup truck with the others and looking at the sky in amazement. I hadn't seen the moon or stars for over a year. It was breathtaking. I fought back tears of joy as I found myself thanking God for something I had taken for granted most of my life.

Milking cows would not have been my first choice had I been given the opportunity, but I was so elated to finally have a few freedoms I became determined to never complain. Life was good. The days went by faster as I put in a full day's work, and I couldn't remember ever sleeping so well. My entire outlook on life improved dramatically in a very short time.

After about three weeks on my new job, I noticed my knees were becoming quite sore from kneeling. This was a dilemma since I had promised myself to never complain. Yet I could not ignore the reality of this nagging discomfort.

I had been watching some of the other guys in the dairy barn and noticed they never had to do the milking. Instead three of them were assigned to shovel manure from a concrete area where the cows walked. They tossed the manure into wheelbarrows, then dumped it in the back where it eventually ended up in a manure spreader. When that chore was finished the inmates spread bales of straw across the barn floor. This was called "bedding down the cows."

I wasn't very excited about the manure part of the job, but compared to the pain in my knees, I began to think bedding down the cows would be somewhat of a promotion. I knew it would be fruitless to complain or to even suggest that I wasn't happy where I was, because of what I'd heard when others made known their discomfort.

"If you can't handle the job, maybe we need to send you back inside."

Not to mention the fact that complaining about a job was a sure way to keep it indefinitely. The guards weren't motivated by such talk. I, however, had a different plan. That night as I lay on my bed, I put in a request to God.

"Lord, I'm not complaining, and I'm not unthankful, so please don't take this the wrong way. I'm very happy to be 'out back' and very happy to be working in the dairy barn, but if there is any way You could work it out for me to bed down the cows, I sure would appreciate it."

And that was all it took. The next day I walked into the barn to milk the cows, when suddenly I heard a booming voice behind me. It was one of the officers.

"Hey, Skinner...you've been milking those cows long enough. I want you to start working with the guys out there and help bed down the cows."

"Yes, sir."

So my aching knee days were over.

Two weeks later, I started asking some of the guys about another position at the dairy barn.

"Who's that guy over there?"

"Oh...that's tractor driver."

"Tractor driver, what does he do?"

"Oh, he just drives the tractor around the farm and delivers eight sacks of feed every day to different locations. As soon as he's finished he takes the rest of the time off and does just about anything he wants. It's the best job out here."

Well that looked appealing so I thought, *Why not?*

That night I gave it a try.

"Lord, You know I'm really happy to be bedding down the cows instead of milking them, and I am very thankful to be outside instead of inside, so please don't take this wrong. If there is any way You could work it out so I could be the tractor driver, I sure would appreciate it."

The next morning as I walked into the barn, the officer in charge called me into his office.

"Skinner, I've been watching you and I'm

happy with how you're working. We have some changes going on around here and your name came up. Do you know how to drive a tractor?"

"Yes, sir. I used to drive one for my grandfather during the summers when I was a kid."

"Great. How would you like to be tractor driver?"

"I'd like that just fine."

"Well, get out there with Joe and he'll show you the ropes."

This was almost more than I could believe. God was really going out of His way. I started thinking, *Maybe I need to ask for some bigger things...like going home.*

Later that night as I lay down again, I said, "Thanks Lord, for the promotion today. It was a very pleasant surprise. By the way, I was wondering—now please don't think I am complaining by any means—but I was thinking it sure would be nice to go home. So if there is any way You could work it out for me to get out of this place and get back to my family, I sure would appreciate it."

No, I didn't wake up and get an immediate release the next day, but there was something in the works that would make a profound impact on my life.

Chapter 21

A Change on the Horizon

When your life is managed by others, and in particular a system, all the days seem to run together. Surprises are rare. But I received a surprise in the mail one day from a friend back home. I expected no more than some small talk in the letter. Actually there was no small talk at all. And it wasn't a letter, but a sermon, specifically a sermon taken from 1 Corinthians, chapter 13, in the Bible.

Somewhere in the midst of reading, the Spirit of God began to speak to my heart. My friend's words had much more than a casual affect on me. Something got to me in a huge way. I found myself sitting on the side of my bed with my eyes so tear-filled I could hardly continue reading.

You see, I had been praying for Randy, my former partner, for over a year. "Lord, please change Randy's heart. Please show him where he was wrong about me. Please help him see what a terrible decision he has made."

Although I was aware of my own mistakes with the business and readily agreed I had done wrong, part of me was angry and hurt by Randy.

I thought he could have handled things better. I thought we could have worked out our differences without getting the attorneys, the courts, and the legal systems involved. If Randy would just forgive me, somehow I would be able to get out of prison.

All of a sudden, in the midst of reading my friend's letter, I found myself overwhelmed with a conviction of my own heart. The Lord began to speak, **"Gary, you've been praying for me to change the wrong person. It's your heart that needs to change. I want you to stop this rotten bitterness you've been harboring."**

"But, Lord, I'm not happy with Randy. He should have worked it out without the courts getting involved. He's handled this all wrong."

"What business is it of yours how he's handled it? The fact is, if you hadn't done what you did, he wouldn't have been put in the position of making a decision, good or bad. You are not locked up because of him. You are locked up because of you, and you alone."

By now I was on my knees next to my bed. It was a serious moment between God and I. The least of my worries was what somebody walking by might think. I had to get my heart right with Him.

As soon as I got honest regarding this matter and confessed my sin, I experienced a sense of huge relief. It was as if a large boulder was lifted from my back. I had no idea I had been holding on to something so destructive and deadly. Even though my circumstances didn't change, my thoughts did. All of a sudden I had an incredibly strong sense that I was going home.

I knew the soonest I could go home was in about two years, because that is when the parole board said they would review my case. Up to this point I didn't believe I would ever get out of there. Up to this point, the best I could accomplish was to get four or five guys to tell me that they "thought for sure I'd get paroled the next time around." But down deep, I didn't believe them. This day, this moment, was different. It was as if something had changed. I thought, *Gary gets to go home next time around.*

A few days later I was sitting outside during a break and feeling exceptionally close to God. All of a sudden He spoke to my heart, **"Gary, I want you to write a letter to Randy."**

"But I don't know what to say."

"I will tell you what to write. After you are finished, I want you to send it to Susan, have her rewrite it in her handwriting and then send it to Randy."

"Lord, is this really You? This doesn't sound right. This sounds like the kind of thing that got me locked up in the first place. It sounds deceitful."

"No, it is not deceitful because what I am going to tell you to write is exactly what I would tell Susan to write if she could hear me. She is overwhelmed with life right now.

She can't hear me clearly. Do as I say and watch what happens."

This was a big step for me in the faith category. Not that I didn't trust God, but I didn't trust my own ability to know if this was Him speaking to me or if it was just some strange idea I conjured up on my own. Yet I felt an urging in my heart. I thought, *What's the worse that could happen? Somebody will send me to jail?*

When a guy is at the bottom of life, it is tough to make him afraid of much. I wanted to do the right thing. I had become weary of mistakes. To make myself feel better about this grand idea, I decided that once it was finished, I would have Susan take it to our pastor to get his perspective on the matter. As I sat down to write the letter, it did not have as much of a "supernatural" feel to it as I had thought it might. In fact, nothing special happened at all, other than the ease with which it flowed out. I do not recall what I wrote, but when I re-read it a couple of times I thought, *Hmmm, this really is how Susan feels.*

I mailed it the next day. As soon as she received the letter, Susan had our pastor read it.

"Susan, I think this is a good thing," Terry said. It really does speak well of how you feel, and I think it is appropriate for you to send it."

So she rewrote the letter and sent it off. Five days later Randy called.

"Hello, Susan, this is Randy. I got your letter and I appreciate what you said. Let's see if we can get Gary out of there. I'd like you to contact the parole board and find out what it would take to get him released."

"Well, they said they won't be reviewing his case again for another two years, so I don't really know what good that would do at this point."

"Why don't you call them anyway and see if there is anything that can be done? In the meantime, I'll talk to the prosecutors office on my end and see what they have to say."

Anyone who knows Susan knows it wouldn't take much for her to make that call. She's a fighter. She will do almost anything to help someone who's in a tough spot, and in the case of that someone being her husband, she was doubly determined.

"Hello, this is Susan Skinner, and I would like to speak to Mr. Evers, the parole board president."

"I'm sorry, Mrs. Skinner, but Mr. Evers isn't here."

"Do you know when he will return?"

"Well, actually, he won't be returning. He retired two weeks ago. Would you like to speak to the new parole board president?"

"Yes, please."

"Let me get Mrs. Jackson on the line."

Susan didn't know it at the time, but this was the greatest thing that could have happened. Mrs. Jackson was the lady who had been my advocate during the first parole board meeting.

"Yes, Mrs. Skinner, I remember your husband's case very well. Let me look at his file and see what might be available. Call me back in a couple of hours and we'll talk about it."

When Susan called back, Mrs. Jackson had some promising news.

"Mrs. Skinner, we are going to make an exception this time. We are going to move up your husband's review. The soonest we can get him on the list is sixty days, which will be January 19th. I'll go ahead and make the arrangements. Maybe we can give you a nice Christmas present."

As soon as Susan told me what Mrs. Jackson said, I yelled, "I'm going home!"

"No, Gary, she didn't say that."

"It doesn't matter what she said, I'm going home!"

The next sixty days were very interesting. I wasn't apprehensive at all. I knew that I knew that I knew, I was going home. I became the topic of interest among many of the guards.

"Hey, Skinner, come over here, I want to talk to you. I hear you are going back to the board again. Is that true?"

"Yes, it is."

"Now why would they do that? You've got another year and a half left before you're supposed to see them again."

"Well, I'm going home."

"Aw, you don't know that. Nobody ever knows. All you know is that you are going to be reviewed again."

"That may be true, but I'm going home."

"How do you know?"

"Because it's time. It's time for me to go

home."

"Well, I hope you're right. I mean it too."

"Thanks."

January 19th arrived and I went before the parole board for the fourth time in a little under a year. I only had to meet with two of the members, not the entire board. I didn't know this until I walked into the room. I kind of chuckled to myself, *Just as I suspected, it's only a formality. They've already made up their minds. I'm going home.*

The two men started by politely asking me to sit down. The board had always treated me with kindness and respect, even when they were giving me the axe.

"Good afternoon, Mr. Skinner."

"Good afternoon."

"Your paperwork says you have a job waiting for you if you are released. Is that true?"

"Well, it was true last April, but to be honest, I'm not sure if that job is still available."

"But your paperwork says you have a job waiting."

"I did then, but it has been several months and I'm not sure if it's still there for me."

"Hmmm. Well, do you think you'll be able to get a job if you get out?"

"I hope so."

"Mr. Skinner, do you think that someday, after you've been out for a while, if you really try, that you'll be able to get a job?"

"Oh, sure."

"Mr. Skinner, it states here you have been in contact with your previous partner and the two of you are on good terms. Is that true?"

"Well, actually, I haven't talked to him myself, but my wife has."

"And everything is good now between the two of you?"

"I'm not 100 percent sure about that, but I hope it is better than it was."

"Mr. Skinner, do you think that when you are released, the two of you can work things out and everything will be good between the two of you *someday*?"

"I hope so."

As I look back it is funny how they almost answered the questions for me to make sure I didn't give the wrong answers. Regardless, the outcome was good and my "shock parole" was reinstated.

As soon as I left the room one of the guards stopped me and asked, "Well, how did it go?"

"They gave me my parole. I'm going home."

He stood there between me and the door for a moment, and at first I wondered what he was thinking. He held out his hand and smiled, "You know Skinner, we're all very happy for you. Congratulations!"

I thought, "I've never seen that kind of response in here before."

I guess, when a guy has favor, it filters through the ranks. As I think about it, I actually did have a lot of favor with everyone, both the guards and the inmates. What I didn't see was that I also had the favor of God with me, in spite of myself. In my humble opinion, I think this has something to do with my heart. Only God truly knows a man's heart and only He knows the depth of its goodness or badness. I had made a lot of foolish decisions and poor judgments, but in the final analysis, if somebody could have dug deep enough, they would have seen that a glimmer of innocence still remained. Somewhere in my early years a seed of God's nature was planted within me. For the first time in a long time, it became evident to those around me, even if they were prison guards and inmates.

The final two months played out smoothly, and I was released March 19, 1993. I don't remember a lot about the last day except that everybody seemed genuinely happy for me. As jubilant as I felt and as kind as everyone was, I didn't feel sentimental in the least toward the big house or its occupants. A friend of our family picked me up, and I was one happy camper.

My release is probably a poor representation of what things will really be like when I die, but sometimes I think of it in relation to that coming day. Every once in a while I think about dying. Perhaps someone I know has died or some catastrophe has happened and I'm watching the report on television, and it hits me.

I wonder how it was when they breathed their last breath?

Then I usually think about myself and about

how it will be for me on that day. The picture I keep getting is of the day I was released. The air was crisp and fresh. The sun was shining brightly. I walked out leaving my old world behind and heading toward my new one. I never once looked back. I was going home.

Chapter 22

No Substitute for Loyalty

If I were to ask you, "Who is your best friend in the entire world?" what would you say?

Before I fouled my life up I thought I had a lot of friends. When the pressure was on, many of them scattered. However, I could always count on my parents. They were amazing. And there was my friend from college, Dave, who offered to quit his job and move to the town where I was locked up, just so he could visit me. Not to mention his financial support to Susan during my time away. And there were those who did visit me and those who helped out with money from time to time, and of course those who continued to pray for me. But one person stood above them all: my wife, Susan.

I guess it is to be expected that the wife would hang in there. Unfortunately, life doesn't work that way in most of these situations. Every week another guy received divorce papers. Every day, I thanked God Susan had decided to stick with me. Yes, I'm aware of the "well-meaning" friends who encouraged her to get rid of me, and I wouldn't have blamed her one bit. Yet somehow she was able to see deeper than our circumstances. She had not taken our vows before God lightly, "for better or for worse."

As I stated earlier, Susan, in many ways had a tougher time with me being locked up than I did. She had to deal with all the creditors, a never-ending problem in those days. In our phone conversations she would tell me who had called and what they were demanding and how they were responding to her answers. None were sympathetic. Many seemed to take it personally that she was unable to pay them at the moment. There just wasn't enough money to go around. The worst was when she would get a "surprise" call from some credit card company she didn't know we had a loan with.

"Gary, I just got off the phone with such-and-such a company and they said you had a credit card with them and you owe them over $2,000."

"Oh, yeah, sorry, I forgot."

"You forgot? How could you forget you owed a company $2,000?"

"I know this isn't the answer you would like to hear, but the fact is, I really did forget. Under my current circumstances I'm not thinking very well."

I realize it sounds lame, but I really did forget. Somehow those companies and the money I owed didn't seem important enough to remember.

Susan had not been working when I went to prison and was trying to get back into the workforce, but it took some time to get into something she could make a decent living at. She considered getting her teaching certificate reinstated, but that didn't seem to be the best option. Nor did she want to apply for a broker's license in Colorado. She hated that business, not to mention the fact her husband was a convicted felon doing time, which might hinder the process. Finally, she decided to get licensed in Colorado as a dental hygienist, a profession she had been in several years prior to me meeting her. The biggest drawback was it would take five months to accomplish.

In the meantime Susan took on more than one job at a time. At first she worked as a waitress during the week and taught skiing at a local resort on the weekends. Actually, it wasn't all that local. She had to drive almost three hours each way. After she got certified as a dental hygienist, she worked for two different dental offices in addition to her other jobs.

Susan had to sell our house, sell a lot of our furniture and other household items, and get some help with moving. We sold the Mercedes before I was locked up, and after my sentence she had to let our new van go back to the dealership. Choices were limited. In the midst of all the hassles, she too had to deal with the embarrassment and shame of her husband's actions. She had to face our friends and relatives, alone. Sure, I was locked up and it was no party, but everybody I looked at was in the same mess.

I heard about her struggles, but I couldn't do much about them. Susan was on her own. It is a miracle she didn't develop any bitterness toward me. In fact, she was incredibly optimistic through the entire ordeal. She never lost sight of her belief that God had brought us together and He had a plan for our lives as husband and wife. To this day I do not know how she remained so hopeful.

From the moment I told Susan about the lies I had lived in the business, until the moment I was released from prison, she stood by me faithfully and weathered whatever disappointments came with a determined strength. I know God sent her to me because there is no possible way I could have found such a friend and companion on my own. She truly is a gift.

Susan also took on the responsibility of raising my son at a most difficult time in his life. Todd seemed to outgrow clothes and shoes as fast as she bought them. He had his own troubles of growing up without dad around. In many ways Todd and Susan had similar temperaments, which caused some interesting moments of friction between them.

He had called her "mom" almost from the beginning of their relationship, but in reality, Susan had only been in that role for a little over four years. Yet I never heard her say anything derogatory toward Todd or myself.

I wonder if she would have married me if in advance she were told, "By the way, after you've been married for four years you will find out your husband has been involved in some illegal business activity, and he will go to prison. You will lose everything—your house, your cars, your reputation, and your retirement. Oh, and while he is lying around "doing time" you will have to take on as many as five jobs at once just to survive. You will have to move twice and almost nobody will help. When the dust clears you will be more than $500,000 in debt and you will lose some friends who think you are an idiot for sticking with Gary. And one other thing, you will have the responsibility of raising his son while he is locked up."

As much as I love me and know what a great guy I am down deep, there is no way I would have married me. Of course, Susan didn't know any of this ahead of time. Good news for Gary.

Along with all of the things I've mentioned, Susan had to also deal with lawyers and prosecutors and judges and parole boards and all the fallout that accompanies such a fight. In the midst of this, she knew the person she was defending was guilty and deserved punishment.

There are no words to describe how much I love her. And though she has her weaknesses just like everybody else, I have absolutely no desire to change her. I love her just the way she is.

Often she asks things like, "Gary, do you like my hair up or down? Do you like it short or long? Do you like my brown shoes or my black ones with this dress? Do you prefer that I wear this dress or would you rather I wore these slacks? Do you like this new lipstick? Do you like this new perfume, or would you rather I keep using what I've been wearing? Do you like the color I've picked for our living room? Do you think we should have more plants in the house? Would you like to go out or stay in for dinner tonight?"

My response? "I don't care."

I realize this is the wrong answer, but it is an honest answer because it's true. I don't care. It is not important to me. Susan is my wife, my friend, my lover, my companion for life. She is God's gift to me and I'm not interested in her hair up or down, or the color of the living room or any of the other things she might want my opinion on. They are trivial to me. Whatever she thinks is best is honestly fine with me. They don't matter. Susan matters.

Lately I have begun to give her some answers because I figured out I was frustrating her with my seemingly "lack of interest" attitude. It is not that I have no interest; it is that I am happy with whatever makes her happy. Since I realized she wants me to have an opinion, I've tried to work myself up to have one, but between you and me, if she asks what I like and then does something completely opposite, I'm just as content.

I could go on and on about how great Susan is and how wonderful it is to be married to her, but it would only be interesting to her and I, so I'll save it. My point is that Susan is a huge part of my life and I don't know how I would have gotten through what I've gone through without her, nor can I comprehend the joy she brings to my life every day. I hear a lot of rotten stories about some rotten marriages and I know I failed miserably on my first. But I doubt many relationships have gone through as much as Susan had to put up with, so forgive me if I fall a little short on "understanding" those who feel like their problems are "just so difficult."

I don't believe Susan always had a good "feeling" about me. I doubt if in those most difficult days she could have honestly said she was "in love." Yet she remained loyal to do her part in fulfilling her commitment before God. Some days love is not a feeling but a decision. No, she didn't trust me. I didn't give her any reason to trust me. But she trusted God and that is what it boils down to for all of us. Will we trust Him?

The Bible talks about how each of us will stand before God and give an account of how we've lived our lives. I know Susan would be quick to tell you there are some things in her life she is not proud of, things she wishes she had handled differently; but regarding how she responded to me and the circumstances forced on her, she can stand unashamed. What an incredible gift I've been given.

Chapter 23

Starting Over

When I got out of prison, I flew home to Colorado Springs and was greeted by a few friends, Todd, and Susan. Our family had survived.

Yes, I was one of the more fortunate ones. Many of the guys did not have any family or even one friend to greet them when they were released. A change of clothes, $75, and you're on your own. I remember some of the guys said they didn't have a clue as to what to do when they got out. One guy had been in several times for petty theft. When asked about his plan he said, "Plan? Who has a plan? I'll just do the best I know. I'll try to make it work this time, but if the pressure of living on the outside becomes too difficult, I know exactly what to do to come back."

I felt badly for him. Unfortunately, guys like him are more in the majority than we would like to believe. Some of them have been in the system over and over again since they were juveniles. In this man's case, he was about to turn fifty, yet had not lived more than three or four consecutive years of his life outside of prison since he was a teen.

On the drive home from the airport, I felt

some hesitancy about our living arrangements. When Susan and Todd needed to cut their expenses, a wonderful family offered to let them move into the family's walkout basement for almost next to nothing. That is where they were living when I was released. I wasn't sure how this would work out with me added to the guest list. All of those fears, however, were put to rest as soon as we met. They welcomed me as if I were one of their own.

They had two young boys, and though the house was on five acres, there were times when it seemed a little small for the two families. We tried to keep things separate most of the time by staying downstairs. We didn't want to overstep their hospitality, yet because of the way the house was set up, we did need to share the kitchen and dining area. Several times over the next year, their hospitality went far beyond what would be expected by anyone. They often invited us to have dinner with them. I doubt they were aware of how frequently we wouldn't have had much to eat had they not offered.

My plan was for us to stay a couple of months and then get a place of our own. It took longer than I'd hoped. After a year, the family moved to Texas and we took over the whole house. Then they moved back, and we returned to the basement. But six months later Susan, Todd, and I were able to get into a nice rental home. I guess you could say we mooched off of these dear friends for a total of two and a half years. Now that's what I call friends.

One of the first things I pursued after coming home was a job. It didn't matter to me what I did. What mattered was that I was working as soon as possible. Getting up early, working hard all day, and sleeping well at night were some basic foundations I wanted to establish again. So when our friend John offered me a job working construction for him, I jumped at the opportunity.

It was funny in a way, because there I was, thirty-eight years old, starting over in a business that was very demanding physically. He assigned me to a framing crew, and since I had absolutely no experience, the lead man kept me very humble. I was about two weeks into this job before they let me use a saw or a hammer. My primary function was "gofer."

"Hey, Skinner, move that pile of lumber by the road up here next to the foundation."

"Hey Skinner, hand me some nails."

"Hey Skinner, hold that wall up while I secure it."

I was grateful to have a job—even at $6.50 an hour—but I struggled some with being bossed around. I tried to remain steady and thankful. I told myself, *Gary, it could be a lot worse. You need to be faithful and glad you have a job and do the best you can. This won't last forever. They will eventually give you more responsibility and increase your pay. Just stay steady.*

Sure enough, after I'd been there two weeks, I was assigned more challenging tasks and received a raise. It wasn't much, but every little bit helped.

Within a year I was making $9 per hour. John pulled me aside one day and said, "Gary, you are doing a great job and you are welcome to stay here and work for me as long as you want. But you need to know I am paying you about as much as I ever will. No matter how good you get, $9 is the top of the pay scale for this kind of work. You might want to start looking around for something that pays better. Like I said, you are welcome to stay here as long as you like, but if I were you, I'd keep my eyes open for something that might offer a better future."

What a great boss. As I look back, I probably could have moved ahead sooner into other kinds of work that paid higher wages, but at the same time, those were days of readjustment to society and internal struggles. It was very therapeutic for me to work hard and sleep well. I did, however, take John's advice and began looking at other options. The first one that came up was an opportunity to work in a window cleaning business. I joined on as a subcontractor and my wages jumped to $16 an hour.

This was an important leap for us. Susan was working in the dental office, earning decent wages, and now with my new job, we had hopes of getting on a better path financially. Of course there was one large glitch. We owed a little over $500,000. I realize this may not be as overwhelming to some people as it was to us, but that's relative. If we had brought home a few hundred thousand dollars a year, our debt would have been manageable. However, with our income bracket, sometimes just the awareness of the debt swallowed up any hope of life getting better.

We owed about $126,000 to the Internal Revenue Service, $36,000 to our friend Tom, over $300,000 to my former partner, Randy, and more than $40,000 for a handful of miscellaneous debts. The IRS situation was unfair. They were convinced the money taken from the business was income, even though I showed them through a paper trail that it was not income and all of it had gone back into the business. We haggled, we argued, we haggled some more, but they stuck to their original decision. The IRS did agree to a minimal monthly payment of $200. I figured up the penalties and the compounding interest, I realized I would have to pay them $200 a month for the rest of my life. *Oh, well,* I thought, *it's better than prison.*

I agreed to pay Tom a small monthly sum with the hope that after a few years I would be able to increase the payment and pay him off. Tom was a good friend. I regretted not being able to pay him more, sooner.

Finally there was Randy. One stipulation of my release was paying Randy $1,000 a month. Because of the agreement, I made the payments, but it did not diminish the temptation I had at times to not pay, especially when money was tight. Even so, the driving factor of honoring our arrangement was my agreement with God. About a month before I got out of prison, God spoke to my heart.

"Gary, there is something you need to know. When you are released from prison you will also be released from your debts. The paperwork will state that you must pay Randy, but nobody will enforce it. It is up to you to walk in obedience to Me. Your responsibility is to Me, not Randy or anyone else. Therefore, I want you to pay everyone back the money they lost in this ordeal—either in full or until, of their own free will, they release you from your obligations. And you had better not try to motivate them to let you off the hook."

We can fool a lot of people, but we can never fool God. He knows our hearts. He knew me well. God knew my past ways were ones of manipulation. He was working on my heart to be honest with Him, those around me, and myself. This little talk He gave me was critical for my future in learning to stay clean and learning to live a truly changed life. Funny thing, it only took a week after being released for my heart to be challenged in a significant way.

On the outside I had to report to my parole officer for one year; then I would be completely free from the system. I'll never forget that first meeting. I walked into his office. He had me sit down in a chair across from his desk and he began a little speech. "Well, Gary, the success of your parole is totally up to you. You can make this easy or you can make this difficult. I only need to see you once a month, and all you need to do is stay out of trouble and show up on time. Your record says you don't have any prior violations. Under the circumstances there is nothing I see in your paperwork or in your demeanor that indicates you are a threat to society. I've looked over your requirements and responsibilities. It states you have agreed to pay your former partner $1,000 per month. Is that how you understand this?"

"Yes, it is."

"Well, let's get something straight right now. There is only one person who can send you back to prison for a violation of your parole and that person is me. Your former partner cannot, and nobody else in the system can. It is me and me alone. I am the only person you need to keep happy. I personally think this agreement is bogus. Frankly, I don't care whether you pay him or not. I am more interested in you getting a fresh start and taking care of your family. So if you decide to pay him, that's your business, but as far as I'm concerned, I will not send you back if you violate this agreement."

"I appreciate that, but I need to uphold the agreement to the best of my ability."

"That is an honorable thing to say, Gary, but don't let this get in the way of your life. As far as I'm concerned, you've paid your debt to society with your time in prison. From my view, your partner should have either cut a deal before you were incarcerated or cancelled the debt upon your release."

"Taking care of this is a lot bigger than I can explain to you right now, but thank you for your concern."

"Okay, I'll see you next month. Here's my card. If you need to talk to me about anything, feel free to give me a call. Good luck."

In a way, his comments were a big relief, but in reality, they didn't mean much because of my agreement with God. This was a very important lesson for me to learn. Obeying God rather than man is more than a "noble attribute." It is the very foundation of a relationship with our Creator. We will not know God's heart until we obey Him. We actually will not truly know a depth of love for Him—or the depth of love He has for us—until we learn obedience.

I was so pleased when we moved out of our friends' basement and into a home of our own. Although it was a rental property, it was a very nice house. It felt good to be in this new place, and once again, we felt a fresh hope for the future. In fact, right after this move I had a talk with God.

"Well, Lord, it feels like everything is going to be okay. We've just moved into a house, our income is holding on pretty well, we are learning how to manage the debt from month to month, and I'm feeling optimistic. I realize we have some large debt, but I think if I continue to stay steady, I will be able to make more money than I am now. Todd is going to college next year, so Susan and I will be empty nesters. Who knows, maybe in a couple of years we could even buy our own house and have some barbecues in the backyard, and maybe even take a vacation. As bad as it's been, it looks like our lives might work out after all."

Soon a new opportunity came my way. The owner of the company I worked for had a friend who was in a car accident. The friend lived in Denver, owned a window cleaning business, and needed someone to help him out for a couple of months while he recovered. My boss told me if I was interested I should give his friend a call. So I did. I discovered I could earn between $200 and $300 a day. I started work immediately. I thought it would be temporary, but the job ended up lasting over two years.

Shortly after transferring to Denver, I had an encounter with God that, once again, impacted my life forever. I was driving toward a small town in the mountains on Highway 70, minding my own business, listening to a tape of a Bible teacher. Since Denver was an hour from where we lived in Colorado Springs, I had quite a bit of driving each day. To help pass the time, I often listened to teaching tapes that Susan gave me. I don't recall the speaker of this particular tape, but I do remember distinctly what was said.

"So, you think you've got life figured out, don't you? In fact, everything is going pretty well for you. The kids will be off to college in a year or so and it's just going to be the two of you. Sure, you'll have your nice house with your nice yard. You'll have some barbecues and maybe you'll take a vacation once in a while. It's turned out all right hasn't it? Well, I'm here to tell you this is not what God had in mind for your life. He didn't bring you into this world to have a nice little existence. You have a call on your life and He's waiting for you to step up to the plate and get busy about His plan for you!"

I pulled over to the side of the road with my face in my hands, crying. It was as if God Himself was speaking to me through that tape deck. All I could think about was the night when I was ten years old and I went forward for that preacher to pray for me. What a terrible mess I'd made of my life.

"Lord, I don't know what to say. You know I am sorry for how I've lived my life. What do You want me to do? What can I do? I feel so foolish. Can You use me? All I have to offer is this wasted life. I've been divorced, I've been in prison, I'm over a half-million dollars in debt, and I have nothing to give You. I want to say that I'm Yours and I'll go and do whatever You want, yet I am embarrassed that I'm coming to you with nothing. Can You use this pile of trash? Lord, I'm so tired of living life my way. I want to do it Your way. If You want me to wash windows the rest of my life, I'll do it. If You have something else in mind, I'm Yours."

After a few minutes I was able to pull myself together and go on about my day. I did not hear

God speak to me. It was very similar to the day I was in prison when I said, "Lord, if it's just You and me, it's okay."

I did not have any sense of His favor or closeness or that He was even paying attention. I did sense, however, that I had once again responded perfectly to the situation. Following this encounter I started making some changes. I told Susan we needed to find a good church and find out where God was calling us. I talked to my parents and asked them to forgive me for my rebellious heart toward them and the decisions I had made. Even though we were on very good terms by then, I had never honestly and humbly asked for their forgiveness for dropping out of college, for marrying Reva without their consent, and for shaming them with my illegal activities. My apology was way overdue. That set in motion something beyond my wildest expectations. The curse was off.

Chapter 24

Called Again

From that day forward I sensed a favor take over the circumstances of my life. Although things had been going well since my release from prison, there was something distinctly different. I personally believe it was connected to two things: a complete reconciliation with my parents and a heartfelt commitment to live a life of obedience toward God.

I believe that as nice as I was externally and as innocent as I was in much of my life, a foundation of rebellion had formed in my heart. That foundation cracked that day in the car on the road to Denver. The moment it did, the curse was broken, and the evidence became very clear.

Almost right away, our financial condition improved. I had talked with several "authorities" about the IRS, including a couple of attorneys, but nobody seemed to have a good answer. Two weeks after my change of heart in the car, my boss asked me a question. "Gary, I'm not trying to be nosy, but I sense you are working through some tough circumstances, and I just wanted you to know if you ever want to talk about them, I'd be happy to listen."

"Well, it's not like it's a secret, so yes, if you are interested, I don't mind talking about it."

We sat down and I went through the whole story. After I finished he said, "I don't know much about the other things you are dealing with, but I do have an idea regarding this IRS situation. I have a friend who is a tax attorney and I think he could help."

"Thanks, but I've already talked to some attorneys and they say there is nothing I can do."

"This guy really knows the law. It couldn't hurt to get his opinion."

It sounded reasonable enough, so I contacted his friend. Susan and I sat down with the man and explained everything and sure enough, he had some great advice. We had some meetings with him, some meetings with another attorney, a meeting before a judge, and "poof" all but $12,000 of the IRS debt disappeared.

A few months later, another miracle took place. I had been making small payments to my friend Tom for quite a while, but they weren't making much of a dent. One day the phone rang.

"Hi Gary, this is Tom."

"Oh, hi Tom. How are you doing?"

"I'm fine. Listen, the reason I am calling is I need a favor. I need you to stop sending me money. Every time I get one of your checks it doesn't feel right. I don't need this money. Sure, you made some mistakes, but they are in the past, and I don't want this to be a hindrance to our relationship. We are too good of friends for that, so please do me a favor and stop paying me. Let's just forget the whole thing."

I honestly didn't know what to say. It was another miracle. I felt like I was released from some of the shame of my past. In a matter of months, over $140,000 of debt was swept away.

The next event of my restoration took place in a very ordinary way. It was as simple as walking into a church. Susan, Todd, and I had been attending a church close to our home for a few months. Although we liked the people, something didn't seem to click. We decided to check out some other churches.

One was a large church on the north side of town called New Life. Sunday rolled around and we ended up arriving about ten minutes late. Part of me was curious to see why so many people attended this church. The largest church I remember attending had about 500 or 600 people. This one had over 4,500. When we walked in, Susan told an usher, "This is our first Sunday. We want to get as close as we can."

I started to argue with her, but before I could say anything, the usher escorted us down the aisle. He found us three seats about five rows from the front. The worship music blared and everyone was standing and singing without reservation. We had only been there for a few minutes when I turned and said, "Susie, we're home!"

"Yes, we are!"

What happened next is difficult to explain, but I literally felt as though something physically dropped into my heart. It was as if my life was rewinding back to when I was a little boy of ten standing in the church I grew up in. There was nothing similar to these churches. They didn't look the same, or sound the same. What made this new church feel so familiar was that I was where I was supposed to be. I was home. Without really understanding exactly why, I suddenly realized I had been lost, wandering aimlessly for over twenty-two years. Tears started rolling down my cheeks. I experienced a feeling of relief, a feeling of safety, and a feeling of being found. Somehow I had made my way back home after all these years.

I didn't figure it out right away, but later I realized home is not a place or a location or a particular church, or even being with a particular group of people. Home is being where God wants us to be. Where home was for me would not necessarily be where home was for someone else. It was so odd because I was standing in a sea of people I didn't know, singing songs I didn't know, worshiping in an unfamiliar manner, and yet I was completely convinced that we were home.

We immediately became church junkies. Susan, and I attended every service that was available. We'd sit as close to the front as possible and try to soak up everything around us. It was funny in a way. We didn't know anybody. We didn't know anything about the church's doctrine. We didn't even know who the pastor was. In fact the senior pastor, Ted Haggard, was traveling out of the country at the time and we attended five services before we ever saw or heard him speak. I remember my reaction after that first sermon.

"Hey Susie, this church has a pretty good pastor too."

Many things changed in me in those days. My heart became tender again to the things of God. It was as if every sermon pierced my heart in some significant way. I became hungrier and hungrier for God. I wanted everything He had for me. After we had attended New Life for three months, I had another encounter with God.

About halfway through one of Pastor Ted's sermons I sensed God speaking to my heart.

"Gary, I want you to stay after church, right where you are, and wait until everyone is out of the auditorium. I have something I want to talk to you about."

I had never heard God speak to me audibly, so I thought perhaps today was the day. What He spoke to my heart about staying after church was more than a small inclination. I knew it was Him. As soon as the sermon ended, I turned to Susan and said, "You and Todd can go on home. I'm supposed to stay here for a while. I think God wants to tell me something."

I actually thought she might want more of an explanation, but she seemed fine with the one I gave.

"Okay, we'll go on home. You do what you think you need to do."

Finally the last group of people filtered out

the door. I sat for a moment and waited. After a few minutes, God spoke to my heart again. Nothing audible, just a very clear impression.

"Gary, I know you already know this because we've talked about it before. I want to reassure you that all is well between you and Me. All the things of your past are forgiven and you and I are doing just fine. There is another issue I know you have been concerned about lately. In fact, you have been beating yourself up about it quite a bit. You have been wondering if I really did call you into the ministry when you were ten years old. You have been wondering if that really was Me, or if it was just some idea you conjured up in your head. The answer is yes. It was Me. I did call you. And yes, you blew it. Those years are gone and you cannot get them back. However, I have a new call on your life."

"What is it?"

"Oh, you don't need to know. When the time is right, I'll make it so obvious you can't miss it. For now, just know you are exactly where you are supposed to be, doing exactly what you are supposed to be doing. One more thing. You know that man on the platform who was speaking today? He is your pastor. I want you to do everything he says to do."

"But Lord, I hardly know the guy. He seems nice enough, but I don't want to follow a man. I want to follow You."

"I know, and that is why I am telling you to listen to him. I want you to do whatever he says to do."

And so I did. Every Sunday I sat near the front with my pen and paper and took notes. Whatever Pastor Ted said to do, I did.

When he said, "You need to develop a lifestyle of praise and worship," I did.

When he said, "You need to develop a lifestyle of prayer and fasting," I did.

When he said, "You need to walk through your neighborhood and pray blessings over your neighbors," I did.

When he said, "You need to tithe," I did.

I didn't argue or debate, analyze or complain. I concluded if I really did hear from God, then my obedience would bear fruit. I began to notice Pastor Ted was coaching the congregation on how to make wise decisions; how to know, love and obey God; and how to live life well. As I followed his instructions, I was amazed at how quickly things changed and how deep my personal walk with God became. It wasn't that Pastor Ted had a corner on God; rather these were all things I had not implemented in my life. They were basic biblical principles taught in churches everywhere.

Yes, Gary became hungry and desperate to get things right in his life.

Chapter 25

Restoration

Shortly after this dialogue with my Creator I entered into a unique season of my life. I realize I have already caused some of you to start scratching your heads with regard to some of my spiritual experiences. What I am about to say will probably challenge you even more. Yet I believe strongly that to glaze over this time of my life would be a mistake. So I've decided to risk being misunderstood.

It began one evening when I was frustrated with myself. I felt like I knew a lot about God, but I didn't really know Him. I decided to press in to get some help from Him. I went to an empty room in our house, lay down on the floor, and began to converse.

"Well, Lord, here I am. Are You here? It doesn't feel like You are. Lord, I'm laying here because I'm trying to connect with You. I heard somebody talk about getting on his face before You and he was able to get near You. Well, here I am. He said to get on our faces and worship You. Is this worship? I'm on my face. He said we needed to humble ourselves before God. Is this humble? I'm really trying."

Tears began to trickle down my face.

"Jesus, how can I know You? I did all the right things for so many years. I read my Bible, I prayed, I memorized Scripture, I went to Bible studies and classes and churches and tried to do all the things they said a good Christian should do. There must be something more. I don't think I know You. Jesus, I want to know You. Will You teach me about You? Will You teach me how to become like You? The Bible says You prayed that we would all become one with You, just as You are one with the Father. I want that. I want to become one with You. Please answer this prayer. Lord, will you change me? I want to be free from everything I am in bondage to. Will You make Yourself known to me?"

And that's how it began. I lay on my face for over two hours, praying, listening, waiting, and weeping. It was incredible. I decided to become desperate for Him. I continued doing this three to four nights a week, for two to three hours each time, for several months. It wasn't always a supernatural session. Sometimes I would lie there and not have any sense of God's presence at all. Sometimes I would fall asleep. Sometimes I would wonder if I was becoming a crazy person. Then, every once in a while, I would have these indescribable times with God. I could sense His presence in a very real way. Sometimes I would feel an electricity flow through my body. Sometimes I would become stuck to the floor as if I were glued there. Sometimes it was as if I could feel

God breathing on me. I never saw God. I never heard Him speak audibly.

It did not matter to me whether I could sense His presence or not. He didn't owe me an experience. I decided to keep meeting with Him whether He made Himself known or not. And I did, week after week, month after month. And He started to rewire me. I began to see significant changes in the way I lived and the way I thought. Attitudes, habits, fears, bondages to sin, shame, and depression began to disappear. He was making me into a new person.

Let me assure you, I am still a work in progress. Just ask any of my friends, or Susan. They will be quick to tell you, "Gary still has changes to make."

Yet I am different. I have changed. I don't think the way I used to think or act the way I used to act. What is so amazing to me is that it has not been a difficult road. It has been and continues to be easy, because all I do is let God have His way in me. Yes, at times I am still weak and foolish. I think they call it "human."

I am not telling you this to promote some kind of new method or system for knowing God. I don't think it was necessarily about me getting on the floor. It had to do with a hunger in my heart and a desperation to know Him.

From that time on, it seemed as though Susan and I grew more and more into the favor of God. We did better financially. The IRS debt was behind us and our debt to Tom was behind us. Shortly after this Randy called and reduced what we owed him to a manageable $36,000. We were only three years away from becoming totally debt free. Besides this I was able to start my own window cleaning business, and it netted $92,000 annually by the second year.

There were only two loose ends left. The first was something I had been praying for every day for over fourteen years, and to be honest, I had lost confidence of seeing it happen. But then, the phone rang.

"Hello, Dad? This is Shannon."

I was caught by surprise. I hadn't heard from Shannon for several months, and when we did talk, it was still the same "distant, unsure, awkward" communication. I immediately started scrambling in my mind, hoping I would have the right words to say, hoping I could somehow connect with her.

"Dad, the reason I am calling is that something has happened with me and I knew it would be important to you. I recently rededicated my life to God. So has my husband and so have the kids...and...well...I love you Dad and I want to be a part of your life again."

I was overwhelmed. I couldn't contain my tears.

"I love you too, Shannon. I never stopped. You've always been a part of my life."

Over the next several months we called each other about twice a month. God supernaturally healed literally years of hurt. Somewhere around the second month of making these calls I picked up the phone. "Hello, Shannon?"

"Oh, hi Dad. Guess what? I was just getting ready to mail you a letter. Since I have you on the phone right now, why don't I just read it to you instead?"

"Sure."

"Dear Dad, I wanted to write and tell you..."

She went on and on about how much she loved me, and how she looked up to me over the years. She reminisced about all the great times we had together and the fun we had shared. I didn't remember those times until she reminded me about them. Whenever I thought of Shannon, I only remembered my failures. All she kept reading were memories about the good times and her respect for me. Then came the clincher.

"Dad, I adore you."

I practically dropped the phone. God had really done it now. After all those years—years of prayer, years of wondering, years of regret. It had seemed so long, so hopeless, so futile. Yet God had been busy in ways I couldn't see. I got my little girl back.

Fortunately for me, there were weeks and sometimes months in between these incredible miracles. If they had happened all at once I don't think I could have managed it. Literally everything in my life turned around for good. What is interesting is that I didn't find joy and peace as a result of being released from prison or being forgiven the debt or even having relationships restored. Those changes had already taken place in the midst of my difficulties. I had learned how to find joy while still in prison. I had learned to find peace when my life was upside down. The good things that followed were just extras, bonuses, icing on the cake.

This is why it was not that big of a deal when I made my final payment to Randy. Many have asked, "Gary, what did it feel like to make that last payment? How did it feel to finally be out of debt?"

"Oh, it felt okay."

"Okay? Just okay? Surely it must have been an exciting moment."

"Don't take this wrong, because I was very glad, but the truth is, all those issues were settled months before. My issues got settled on my face, on the floor, in times of prayer and fasting, in times of quietness before God. That was when I was set free. Not when I made my last payment."

My business continued to prosper. I even put together a plan to expand to three times the size over the next couple of years. Two weeks later, everything took another turn.

While standing at the top of a twenty-foot ladder, washing windows, my pager went off. It was Russ, one of the pastors from church. As soon as I could get off the ladder, I called him back.

"Hello, Russ? This is Gary. You paged me?"

"Yes, thanks for getting back to me. Gary, I need you and Susan to come to my house this evening. I want to talk to you about something."

We went to his house about 7:00. His wife, Courtney, greeted us at the door, and we all sat down in the family room. Russ had a big grin on his face. I could tell he was having some fun with this.

"Well, what is this all about?"

"Gary, I would like your permission to submit your name to Pastor Ted and the executive staff for the possibility of hiring you. I'd like you to assist me with leadership training and development."

"Are you serious? Is this some kind of joke?"

"No, Gary, this is not a joke. I am very serious."

"But Russ, you know my history, you know my background, you know all about me. There is no way this could work out."

"Listen, some of us on the church staff have been discussing this. We've watched your life and we believe you are the right person for the job."

"I don't know, Russ. I'm honored, but it doesn't seem like the right time. I'm not sure if I'm ready. I don't think I'm qualified for this large of a responsibility. I haven't had any training."

"I'll be there for you, I'll help you learn."

"I'd love to say yes, but this would be a very big step for me."

"Okay, Gary, how about this. Why don't you pray about it over the weekend? Pastor Ted won't be able to meet with you until next week anyway. In the meantime, at least agree to go through the process, and if it doesn't work out, no harm done. Does that sound fair enough?"

"Okay, I'll agree to go through the process."

After we went home that night I was an emotional wreck. Part of me wanted to believe this was God working, but another part was very cautious. I thought, *What if this isn't from God? What if this is just a setup for me to fail again? After all, life is going very well these days. Could this be a well-meaning idea that would actually throw me back into financial trouble? I know what the church pays and it is nowhere near the six figures that I'm on track to earn by next year*.

I couldn't sleep. I was more than a little restless. I decided to give Susan a break from my tossing and turning.

"Susie, I'm going to go to the spare bedroom. I might not get to sleep for a while."

I lay down in the next room and stared at the ceiling. My mind continued to race.

"Lord, is this You? Is this Your idea? Is this what You meant when You said You would make it so obvious I can't miss it? Or am I getting ahead of You? I don't want this if it is not Your idea or if it is the wrong timing."

I waited for Him to respond. Nothing.

"Lord, it doesn't make any sense. First of all, Ted is not going to go for it. I don't think I measure up to his standards for a position in ministry. What should I do, Lord? Please talk to me."

Still nothing. Apparently God was in China for the evening. I didn't sleep a wink. I looked at my watch and realized I had better get up. I had a plane to catch because I was going to visit my parents for the weekend.

"Well, Lord, I guess You're not talking to me just yet. Just so You know, I'm ready whenever You are."

I got cleaned up and was almost ready to walk out the door when I sensed the presence of God in a significant way. If felt like He was about three inches from my face. I didn't see anyone, but I could feel something. He spoke very strongly to my heart.

"Gary, I don't care if you mess up the interview next week. I don't care what you say or what you do. In fact, I don't care if you make a complete fool of yourself, but don't you dare mess this up because of the money."

That was all the reassurance I needed. That was why I couldn't sleep all night. I was worried about the money. He knew my heart. I had to smile.

I left for the airport, visited my parents, and came back Monday afternoon. I was about to call Russ to make sure everything was set for Tuesday when all of a sudden I remembered a dream I'd had a couple of years prior. In this dream I was standing in Pastor Ted's office, and he was sitting at his desk. He said, "Gary, I don't have a problem with you. I think you're a great guy, but the truth is, with your past history, I don't think it is best for the church."

And then the dream ended. I thought, *Maybe my dream will come true. Well, that's okay. Maybe*

God wants me to go through the interview process to see if I'll be obedient. I wonder how much Ted knows about me? This has got to be clean.

I called Russ.

"Russ, how much does Pastor Ted know about my past?"

"He knows the big points."

"Listen, I want him to know everything. I don't want him to hire me and then six months later decide I'm not the right person for the job because of the foolishness I've been through. I'm going to tell him everything tomorrow."

"Gary, that won't be necessary. We have told him about your past."

"Even prison?"

"Yes, even prison. He said that he wasn't interested in where you've been. He said he's only interested in where you are now and where you are headed for the future."

"Okay, then, I won't bring it up. I just want this to be done right."

"It's going to be fine. I'll see you tomorrow at eleven."

I went to bed Monday night relieved that I didn't have to go through my whole story the next day, though I was prepared to do so.

Finally the moment arrived. I walked into Pastor Ted's office. He looked at me, paused, then smiled, and said, "I've seen you around here before."

I had to chuckle inside. He had no idea how much of an impact his life and sermons had made on me over the past two and a half years. In fact, he didn't even know me.

"Have you had lunch yet? I'm hungry. Let's grab a bite to eat and we'll talk over lunch."

Pastor Ted, Russ, and Ross, another associate pastor, all drove together and I followed in my truck. We went in the restaurant, sat down, and the interview began. Pastor Ted only asked me four or five questions. I couldn't tell if he liked my answers or not. But, it didn't really matter. God already told me I could mess up the interview. Overall it seemed like it went well.

Then Pastor Ted said, "Okay, Gary, that should do it. Russ will give you a call within a couple of weeks to let you know what we've decided."

I thanked them for their time and went on about my day. About ten minutes later my pager went off. It was Russ. I gave him a call.

"Well, Gary, he wants you. Come on in and sign the paperwork and we'll get you started."

I couldn't believe my ears. The impossible had happened. This was the last loose end in my life. After all these years, all the pieces had come together. Well, sort of...

Chapter 26

One Small Glitch

At first I didn't completely know what my responsibilities at the church would be. All I knew was I would be working with Russ and his team. A few weeks into my new job I faced a difficult challenge. I was sitting in my office when Russ walked in, laid a piece of paper on my desk, and said, "Gary, you need to fill this out as soon as possible and get it back to me."

I looked at the top of the page. It read, "Application for Licensing as a Minister."

It had several blanks for common answers such as name, address, and so forth. I looked further down the page to where the questions were.

1. Have you ever been divorced?
2. Have you ever filed bankruptcy?
3. Have you ever been arrested?
4. Have you ever been convicted of a felony?

"Russ! This is not going to work! What is this all about anyway?"

"Pastor Ted wants you to get licensed. You are already doing the work of a pastor; he wants to make it official."

"But I've got the wrong answers on all of these.

This is not a good idea."

"Don't worry about it. Just fill it out and write some explanations on the back."

"There's not enough room."

"Then write on a separate sheet of paper."

"Why do I have to do this? Is it really that important?"

"Gary, it's not a big deal. It's basically a formality. You'll fill it out, you'll meet with the elder board, and then you'll be licensed."

"Elder board! That doesn't sound good."

"Don't worry, I'll be there with you and help you explain. It's going to be fine."

"I don't like this."

I filled out the paperwork and turned it in the next day. I found out that I would be meeting with the elder board within a month.

Just when I thought everything was going well.

A few days later, Russ called me into his office.

"Gary, there is something I need to tell you. I'm leaving. I'm moving to Mississippi to work for a friend of mine. We are putting our house on the market and we leave next week to look around for housing possibilities down there."

"Next week! Who's going to teach me what to do around here? What about my interview with the elders? This is very poor timing."

"Oh Gary, you'll be okay. You already know what to do. Just step out and do it. As far as the elder board is concerned, I'll write a letter of recommendation."

I didn't say much after that, but a sick feeling

developed in my stomach. This had all the ingredients of a disaster.

So Russ and Courtney put their house up for sale. I think it sold in two weeks. They found a place almost immediately in Mississippi. It felt as though they were whisked away overnight.

I became very unsettled. Finally the day arrived for me to meet with the elders. As I looked around the room, I realized only a couple of them knew me. Nobody smiled. I tried to lighten up the moment by making a funny comment.

"Wow, the last time I felt like this, I was sitting in front of the parole board."

Nobody laughed.

I thought, *This might be more like the parole board than I thought. I better straighten up.*

They asked me several questions. They asked me to tell them about my story, but I only had fifteen minutes. I thought, *Fifteen minutes? That's only enough time to tell the bad parts. This is not a good day.*

I did the best I could under the circumstances. They were kind to me, but I didn't leave the room with a good feeling. I went to my office and tried to mentally process what had just taken place. Pastor Ted walked by and said, "Hey, Gary, come on out here. Let's talk about your interview."

I walked into the next room. He and another pastor who had been in with me during my interview were standing together. Pastor Ted asked, "Well, how did it go?"

"I don't know. It was tough."

The other pastor said, "They decided to put their decision on hold for a month because of how complicated Gary's past is. I think everything will be all right. They will review you again in thirty days."

I thought, *Now there's a familiar phrase.*

Pastor Ted laughed and said, "I'm sure the elders just need some time to think about it."

I went home wondering what would happen if they turned me down. At first I was a little frustrated with how things had turned out, but then I gave it some more thought and changed my conclusion.

"Of course they want to think about it. They should want to think about it. My past is horrific. They are considering entrusting me with a very important office in the church. They should not take it lightly. They should be very careful about this decision."

The next day Pastor Ted walked into my office, closed the door, sat down across from me, and said, "Listen, Gary, it looks like we're going to have a problem with getting you licensed. Very few of the elders really know you and I think we are moving too fast with this. I would like you to sign a paper withdrawing from the licensing. We'll look at this again in a couple of years after the elders get to know you better. It won't affect your job in any way. The only thing it will affect is your title. If you are fine with that, we'll just move on and it will be business as usual. Is that okay with you?"

"Sure. I never asked to be licensed in the first place. I'm not interested in titles."

"Great, I'll have that letter drawn up later today."

Everything was going to be just fine. And it was for about two minutes. But after he left my office, it seemed as if all the demons in hell began screaming in my ears.

"So, you're not going to be a pastor. You must not be good enough. There's not much truth to that forgiveness stuff. The forgiveness of Jesus isn't quite good enough for the church. You'll always be substandard in their eyes. Let's face it, Jesus can forget your sins, but the church can't."

I began to feel sick, so I decided to go for a drive and have a talk with God.

"Lord, what's going on? I thought I was supposed to take this job. I thought this was the fulfillment of Your calling for me. I thought I was walking in obedience. Now this. I really don't care about my title, but something is wrong here. It doesn't feel clean. I feel like Pastor Ted is stuck with me. I feel like he hired me in good faith and now it is all blowing up in his face. I don't like how this is going. What do you want me to do? How am I supposed to manage this?"

"Go back and talk to him. Offer him your resignation. Don't resign, but give him the option. Don't worry. If he chooses to accept your resignation, I'll take care of you. If he doesn't, then at least you've cleared the air."

I drove back to church and asked to see Pastor

Ted. He immediately stopped what he was doing.

"Come on in, Gary. What's on your mind?"

As I entered his office, everything suddenly seemed very familiar. I stood across from him and he sat behind his desk, just like in my dream. Because of the dream, I knew how it would turn out.

"Well, sir, this doesn't feel right. It's not about the title; it's about what is right and best for you and the church. I am concerned that somehow you didn't learn all you needed to know about me before you hired me. It doesn't feel clean. It feels like you are stuck with me, and you are trying to make the best of it. Let's start over. Let's pretend today is the first day you hired me, and you have an opportunity to make the decision all over again. If you think it is best for the church, I'll step down. I just can't work here if it doesn't feel clean."

He waited for a moment and said, "Absolutely not. I do think you are the right person for the job and I think you're going to do great around here. As long as you are okay with not having a title of "pastor," then you and I are good."

"That's all I needed to know. I'm fine without the title. I just wanted to make sure you and I were all right."

And that was the truth. I left his office and all was well.

I did keep my eye out for that piece of paper to withdraw my name, but it didn't come to me that day. In fact, it never did show up. Three weeks later one of the associate pastors told me, "Gary, we need you and Susan to come to the elders meeting this Sunday. Pastor Ted wants to give it another shot."

Susan and I both went to the meeting ready for interrogation number two. They didn't even call us into the room. Apparently Pastor Ted and some of the elders who knew us were able to make a strong enough case for my approval. The licensing went through.

Over the course of the next several weeks, life mellowed out. This was fine with me. Yet it seems like just when I think I've got a handle on things, God pulls another surprise out of the hat and shakes me up. And He did.

The church was holding its annual "Life-Giving Church Conference." More than five hundred pastors and their wives from all over the world came to this particular event. On the third day we closed out with a time of communion. This final session was held in the chapel of the World Prayer Center, which is a part of the New Life campus. It is a large round building with a huge globe that slowly rotates in the front of the chapel. A large bay of windows stretches halfway around the chapel area, which allows a beautiful view of Pikes Peak and the Colorado Rockies.

Pastor Ted had asked some staffers to help with communion that day. We held trays with tiny cups of grape juice or small pieces of bread. While the worship team sang, those in attendance walked single file to the front, took a cup and bread, and returned to their seats. My job was to serve the bread.

The music was incredible and the mood was absolutely perfect. The worship team sang, "What can wash away my sin? Nothing but the blood of Jesus."

All was fine until about halfway through the first verse. Unexpectedly I sensed the closeness of God engulf me. This is a great experience if I am alone. But I wasn't. I was standing up front, serving the bread. And when God shows up, I often cry. I'm not talking about a sniffle here or there, I'm talking about real weeping. This means tears and snot.

As I felt this happening, I started to pray silently and fervently.

"Lord, I sure do love You and I sure do love it when You make Your presence known to me, but this is a bad time."

The feeling increased.

"Lord, please, can we wait until later when You and I are alone? I do not want to fall apart in front of all these people."

This continued for about ten minutes. It seemed like it took an eternity for everyone to get through the line. I did pretty well though. I held the tears back to a minimum and I am happy to report that no snot fell into the plate of bread. Finally the last person walked by. I was able to move somewhat to the side of the chapel, but I was still up front in clear view of the crowd. I needed to stay there until Pastor Ted led us through the rest of the ceremony.

He began by reading some Scripture and then talking about the significance of the cup and the bread. I thought, *Come on, let's get this going. We don't need a whole sermon. These are pastors. They know all about communion. We need to speed this up. I need to blow my nose.*

As he continued to talk, I thought I should come up with a plan. The door was not too far away. But under the circumstances and the reverence of the moment, bolting out did not seem like a good option. Then I got an idea. *If I can keep myself together until he says the final prayer, I can turn and face the windows, and nobody should notice my condition. They will all be thinking of leaving and I can remain up here and deal with this incredible moment.*

I made it. He said the final "amen" and I immediately turned toward the windows facing outside. As soon as I made the turn, it hit. I began to shake and cry like a little boy. The tears streamed and the snot poured: absolutely pathetic. I didn't want to complain because this "presence of God" is an amazingly wonderful experience. I prayed, "Lord, why is this happening right now? What is going on?"

Through my tears I looked down and couldn't believe what I saw. I was no longer wearing a nice suit and tie. I was wearing the exact same clothes I wore my first day in the county jail. I closed my eyes, then opened them again. Those lousy jail clothes were still there. I wondered if anyone else could see how I was dressed. All of a sudden I heard a voice. It was my voice. I actually heard my voice in my ear as clearly as if I were speaking out loud, only I wasn't speaking at all. The words were familiar:

"Well, Lord, I've really done it this time. I've really messed up about as bad as I could. I hate what I've done and I hate who I've become and I hate where I am. Lord, please don't let me die in here. Please don't let this be what I'm known for. Please don't let this be what my wife and kids think of when they think of me. Please don't let this be my legacy."

Immediately I felt like I was being transported to the ceiling of the chapel. I wasn't actually moving, but that is what it felt like. It was a vision. From that high vantage point, I watched myself stand in the front of the room wearing my suit and tie, serving communion to those pastors. Then the Lord spoke to me, almost audibly.

"See what I did?"

Chapter 27

What About You?

Well, it's been several years since that day. I'm still very happily married to Susan, still growing in my walk with God, still experiencing amazing moments in my quiet times with Him. There is no such thing as an "arrival" point. In fact, I believe the process is where all the excitement is. I'm still in process.

Often I will be alone somewhere and my mind will drift back to those days when life was not so grand, when my story was not so promising. Whether I'm thinking about it, writing about it, or talking about it, it always seems the same—I feel like I'm talking about someone else's life. I am not the same man any longer. Hope and joy fill my days, rather than fear, depression, anxiety, anger, stress, and more stress. Instead of loathing each morning, wondering whether I can juggle my bad choices one more day, I have a peace of mind like never before.

Yes, this is my story. But as I warned you in the beginning, this your story too.

No, it is not about being a preacher or a missionary or working in a church. Yet it is about calling and purpose. Everybody has a calling. It is about restoration and healing. Everybody has lost or broken something significant in their lives. It is about failure, disappointment, and shame. Everybody has something they wish they could have done better or differently. It is about forgiveness. Everybody has some relationship that has been strained in this regard. It is about both good and bad decisions and their corresponding reward or consequence. Everybody has experienced both. It is about a personal relationship with a loving and powerful God. Everybody has been separated in some manner from God and either openly or secretly desires to have that relationship righted.

I know God has a plan for you. I know He can restore and heal your circumstance even if it is just to the point of you finding peace in the midst of your loss. You don't have to be brilliant or perfect. It is not about education or training. It's not about size, shape, or color. You see, I'm just an ordinary guy; nothing fancy, nothing slick, just a plain vanilla wrapper. If God can work these kinds of miracles in my life, imagine what He can do in yours. If I can be restored, so can you. If I can hear from God, so can you. All He is looking for is a willing heart to love, trust, and obey Him.

There are basically two groups of people this book was written for. The first are those who have been living life their own way, following their own plan, doing what they want when they want. They have allowed their hearts to become hardened toward the voice of God. The Lord is saying,

"Turn around, you're going the wrong way. I have a better plan for you."

The second are those who God has spoken to in times past. You have had a sense of Him calling you to do something, or perhaps He once inspired you with an idea. You seemed to be closer to Him in those days. You haven't followed through. Time has slipped away. The Lord is saying, **"You're not too old and it's not too late."**

He desires for you to renew your trust in Him. If you will simply begin to take steps of obedience, you will begin to see Him bring about these promises.

There may be some of you who know you are not following God's plan, but you are not ready to change, to get serious, to turn around. You are thinking, *I know I should make the move, but I'm not ready. I'll do it later. I'm not through living life my way.*

Some of you might go so far as to say, "Gary, got his life back on track with God. He didn't get serious until he was in his forties. I've got plenty of time for those kinds of decisions. I'll make things right with God later."

Well, you may or you may not. There are graveyards full of people who have said the same thing and they never lived long enough to see it happen. There are no guarantees. Yes, I got a second chance, but there is no guarantee I'll get another, and there's no guarantee you'll get yours either unless you make the decision right now.

Some of you may be wondering if it's too late

or if you've said "no" one too many times. Or perhaps you think you need to "fix" a few things before you come to Him. Nothing could be further from the truth. God will meet you right where you are. You do not have to prove anything to Him.

I used to have this great dog. She was a beautiful German shepherd, very intelligent, very responsive to learn. She could do all kinds of tricks: fetch sticks and tennis balls, sit, and lie down. One of my favorites was when she would sit in front of me and I'd balance a little treat on her nose. She would sit there for as long as I required, just staring at it.

Then I would say, "Take it."

Immediately she would flip her head and grab the treat in midair.

Yet as beautiful as she looked and as smart as she was, and as much as I loved to have her perform those tricks for my friends and guests, none of those qualities mattered much to me. I just loved her because she was my dog. She often sat next to me and laid her head on my lap. After a couple of moments she would look up with those big brown eyes and let out a deep sigh, as if to say, "It just feels good to be here near you."

That is how I believe we are to be with God and that is how I believe He sees us. He is not waiting for us to perform for him, to accomplish some great feats, or live to impress others. He just wants our hearts. First and foremost He wants us to enjoy being near Him.

Regardless of where you are in life, I want to encourage you to find a quiet place and get honest in your heart with God. He loves honesty. Even if you're hurting or angry or confused, He still loves honesty. Just start talking to Him like you would anyone else. Tell Him what you've been going through. Tell Him what your hurts and struggles have been. Tell Him you are tired of living life your way and you are ready to follow His plan. Tell Him you're sorry for the past. Tell Him you want to love, know, and obey Him. Tell Him you need His help. Take as long as you need until you feel like you've talked it out. Then make some decisions. Every day, decide to do your best to follow Jesus Christ. Be deliberate in taking time to talk to Him and time to listen for His voice. As I've said several times, I've never heard Him speak to me audibly, but I have learned how He speaks to me. His manner or method of communicating to you might be very different than it is for me. He will show you if you'll be patient and open to learn.

The time for you to act is now. The time for you to change your course is now. The time for you to begin fulfilling God's purpose for your life is now. Trust me, you will not be disappointed.

Contacts:

vanilla publishing company
g skinner enterprises inc.
3472 Research Parkway Suite 104
Colorado Springs, Colorado 80920

garyskinner.com